THE HONEY DO LIST FOR GUYS DIY MADE EASY

Tackle Home Projects With Confidence, Better Relationship With Your Partner, Develop Quick & Simple DIY Skills With Ease

BRENT SNIPER

Table of Contents

Introduction

It was a Saturday morning like any other. Tom woke up ready to tackle the ever-growing "Honey Do" list that his wife, Jane, had been keeping on the refrigerator. He made himself a cup of coffee and geared himself up for a day of home improvement projects. First up was installing the new ceiling fan in the bedroom. *Easy enough*, Tom thought to himself. He'd seen it done dozens of times on YouTube. How hard could it be?

Tom started by turning off the power at the breaker box. Using a screwdriver, he removed the old ceiling fan and fixture. After disconnecting the wires, he began installing the new mounting bracket that came with the ceiling fan. So far, so good. As Tom was attaching the wires, he felt a sudden jolt. The power was back on! Sparks began to fly as Tom scrambled to turn the electricity off again. But it was too late—the damage was done. The newly installed ceiling fan crashed down, shattering on the floor. Jane came rushing into the room only to find a shocked

Tom standing there, covered in drywall dust and looking completely bewildered.

While this particular story may be exaggerated, it points to an all-too-common experience for many men—the dreaded Honey Do list. The list of home improvement projects, repairs, and other household tasks frequently assigned to men by their partners can instill a sense of obligation, anxiety, and even resentment (Family Handyman, 2019). But it doesn't have to be that way.

This book provides the necessary knowledge, skills, and mindset to not only complete the Honey Do list, but do it confidently, effectively, and without unwanted stress. By approaching these projects as opportunities to enhance skills, deepen relationships, and take pride in your living space, you can transform chores into rewarding experiences.

Throughout this book, you will learn:

- the significance and psychology behind the Honey Do list
- building confidence in DIY skills
- gathering essential tools for home projects
- strategies for prioritizing and managing projects
- maximizing efficiency through planning and preparation
- fostering teamwork with your partner
- mastering basic home repairs to save money

- improving curb appeal and outdoor spaces
- passing DIY skills to children through bonding projects
- celebrating accomplishments and setting new goals
- transforming the Honey Do list into a rewarding journey
- developing a positive, collaborative mindset around home projects
- learning practical skills to complete tasks like a pro
- strengthening your relationship with your partner along the way

These are the practical strategies for prioritizing and tackling home improvement tasks, while also cultivating a sense of accomplishment, purpose, and greater connection in your relationship. With the right tools, techniques, and perspective, you can become a Honey Do master.

Home improvement projects often strike fear into the hearts of men when assigned by their partners. The dreaded Honey Do list—that seemingly endless list of repairs and upgrades requested by a spouse—has become a stressful fixture in many relationships. Just glance at the statistics:

- Sixty percent of home improvement tasks assigned to a partner go unfinished (This Old House, 2009).
- Seventy-five percent of couples report having an ongoing Honey Do list (Bob Vila, 2021).
- More than 50% of these lists contain more than 10 major projects (My Creative Days, 2023).

Why do so many of these lists remain perpetual works in progress? The reasons are complex, touching on gender norms, confidence gaps, and relationship dynamics.

Traditionally, home maintenance has been viewed as the husband's domain, regardless of actual skill or interest (Liu, 2023). This outdated stereotype pressures men to take on DIY projects alone to prove their "manliness"—even if they lack experience.

Feeling incapable around repairs and improvements can severely damage a man's self-esteem (DIY Daddy, 2019). But developing core competency in home DIY skills is within reach for any willing learner.

Without proper communication and collaboration, these lists become relationship minefields. Nagging and arguments ensue over delayed tasks and forgotten duties. But reframing the Honey Do list as a shared tool for growth brings couples together.

The Honey Do List Unveiled

The Honey Do list has become an infamous fixture in many relationships. Typically created by one partner, it contains a myriad of requested home repairs, upgrades, and tasks for their significant other to complete. But what drives this list and why do tensions often arise? Gaining insight into this phenomenon is key.

While created with good intentions to improve the home, the Honey Do list inadvertently becomes a sore spot for many couples. The partner making the requests takes on the role of identifying and managing tasks, but the recipient feels micromanaged and overwhelmed by the demands.

The sheer length of many couples' perpetual Honey Do lists is telling. One study found the average wife reported more than 130 outstanding items for their husbands to tackle, while only

15% of husbands had issued such lists to their wives (This Old House, 2009). This imbalance can brew resentment.

Making assignments based on gender rather than skill sets or interest is problematic. Men feel undue pressure to handle maintenance considered "masculine" domains, while women are excluded. In reality, skills vary individually, not by gender norms.

Underlying conflicts about financial priorities also influence the list's reception. Partners may clash over allocating budgets for home improvements versus other goals. Big-ticket projects become contentious.

According to psychologist Bella DePaulo, when nagging over a lengthy Honey Do list persists for years in a relationship, marital satisfaction and stability often suffer. The cycle of disappointment erodes intimacy.

With proper communication and collaboration, couples can reframe the Honey Do list as a shared tool for accomplishing mutual goals. But left unchecked, this list can drive partners apart. Recognizing the psychology and pitfalls is the first step.

SIGNIFICANCE OF THE HONEY DO LIST

The Honey Do list—that seemingly endless list of requested home repairs, improvements, and projects assigned by one partner for the other to complete—has become a ubiquitous part of many romantic relationships and family dynamics. However, looking at the high rate of perpetually unfinished or ignored Honey Do projects reveals some deeper significance and complex gender dynamics underlying this common cultural phenomenon.

Several studies highlight the scope of this issue:

- A shocking 60% of home improvement tasks assigned to a partner on a Honey Do list wind up going incomplete or unstarted, according to one revealing survey (This Old House, 2009).
- Another study found that nearly three out of four couples report having an ongoing Honey Do list circulating between them at some point in their relationship (Bob Vila, 2021).
- More than 50% of these relationship Honey Do lists contain more than 10 major home projects ranging from repairs to renovations (My Creative Days, 2023).

These statistics clearly highlight just how incredibly widespread, yet also problematic, the Honey Do list has become in many relationships. But what explains why these well-intentioned lists so consistently tend to remain perpetual works in progress with most tasks lingering undone?

The Imbalance of Emotional Labor

Some relationship experts suggest that the Honey Do list imbalance stems in part from an unequal distribution of invisible emotional and mental labor in the relationship. The partner creating and managing the list takes on the brunt of the

cognitive burden, remembering needs, planning projects, identifying solutions, and prompting action. Meanwhile, the
partner assigned the tasks bears responsibility just for physical
execution. This disconnect can foster resentment on both sides
over time.

Unrealistic Expectations

Hand in hand with the imbalance of emotional labor, the
partner requesting projects may also have unrealistic expectations about their partner's level of skill, interest, available time,
and follow through. Passionate ideas transform into intimidating demands. Partners hesitate to speak up and reset expectations, allowing the list to snowball unchecked.

Conflict Avoidance

On the receiving end, the common tendency to avoid potential
conflict leads many partners to passively accept ever-growing
Honey Do lists regardless of actual bandwidth. Saying no risks
disappointing their spouse and being perceived as unsupport-
ive, even when overwhelmed. This conflict avoidance allows the
list accumulation to continue unchecked.

Gender Stereotypes and Norms

Finally, ingrained gender stereotypes and societal norms
contribute to the Honey Do phenomenon escalating. Home
maintenance and repairs are traditionally perceived as mascu-

line responsibilities. This can pressure men to take on projects, even if disinterested, while dissuading their partners from acquiring those DIY skills themselves.

In summary, the Honey Do list has become problematic and overloaded in many relationships due to imbalanced emotional labor divisions exacerbated by unrealistic expectations, conflict-avoidance tendencies, and stubborn gender norms. But insight into these dynamics provides opportunities to right the course and work together in healthier ways.

Origins of the Honey Do List

The concept of the Honey Do list has its origins in traditional household gender roles and division of labor, where home maintenance tasks and repairs were seen largely as the domain and responsibility of men.

The term "Honey Do list" is believed to have first emerged as shorthand in the 1970s to refer to the list of various household chores and repairs a housewife would routinely assign to her husband in suburban middle-class families (Jezek, 2020).

"Honey, do this..." was a familiar prompt from wives urging their husbands to take care of outstanding household projects and needs around the home. This cultural phenomenon reflected the gendered expectation that male partners should handle domestic repairs and handiwork, while women focused on other homemaking responsibilities.

While societal gender norms and expectations have certainly evolved over recent decades, several surveys reveal the persistence of the Honey Do list dynamic in many modern households and relationships:

- Some 60–85% of husbands report still regularly receiving a Honey Do list of requested projects from their wife or partner, compared to only 15–40% of wives receiving such lists from husbands (Bob Vila, 2021).
- More than 75% of couples confirm having an active Honey Do list circulating at some point in their relationship, though lists given to men remain far more prevalent (Family Handyman, 2023).
- The majority of same-sex couples report creating joint chore lists, avoiding to the gendered Honey Do designation (My Creative Days, 2023).

So, while explicit old-fashioned gender roles have weakened over time, the lopsided prevalence of wives and female partners assigning Honey Do lists to their husbands or male counterparts endures.

The Modern Honey Do List Dynamic

For many modern couples, the Honey Do list continues to serve as a means for one partner (most often the wife/girlfriend) to identify and delegate various household chores, repairs, and home improvement projects that they would prefer their male spouse/partner to complete.

These lists help facilitate discussion and distribution of domestic responsibilities. However, the persistence of Honey Do lists given primarily to men reveals lingering gender biases.

Many women still avoid developing basic DIY skills, defaulting to their male partners for these tasks whether or not they have interest, time, or capability. And social conditioning pressuring men to dutifully accept Honey Do lists regardless of fairness or bandwidth remains strong.

While the origins of Honey Do lists lie in traditional gender roles, conscious examination of lingering biases plus open communication and sharing of DIY skills can help modern couples move toward more equitable partnerships and project collaboration.

Motivations Behind the List

For the partner initially creating and assigning the various home repairs, upgrades, and tasks that comprise the Honey Do list, their motivations often stem from a well-intentioned desire to improve and enhance the home, provide helpful direction for their spouse, and promote a sense of shared domestic responsibility within the relationship (My Creative Days, 2023).

Honey Do lists frequently originate from the inspiration of trendy home-design ideas on platforms like Pinterest, combined with the ever-present pressure to maintain and increase home values through upgrades. The act of creating a Honey Do list can represent a partner's attempt to identify and capture necessary home maintenance work and desired projects.

However, without proper open communication, collaboration, and context provided upfront, these one-sided well-meaning lists of projects and requests can too easily be perceived as demanding, controlling, or even nagging.

Rarely is adequate background conveyed around the underlying motivations for the requests, the desired timeline for completion, or what level of priority each task on the list holds. Partners may also have very different personal tolerances for living with existing home flaws versus an enthusiastic drive to continually upgrade and enhance a space just for enhancement's sake.

For the partner receiving a lengthy Honey Do list full of repairs, upgrades, and other assignments, taking this on can quickly feel anxiety-inducing, overwhelming, and can foster resentment. This is especially true for men who may lack baseline confidence, skills, or knowledge related to successfully completing extensive home improvement and maintenance projects independently (DIY Daddy, 2019).

According to one revealing poll, a whopping 75% of men expressed wishing they had greater competence with basic household DIY repairs and maintenance (This Old House, 2010).

Outdated gender assumptions and stereotypes can further compound the issues surrounding Honey Do lists. The partner creating the list may default to simply assigning what have traditionally been viewed as a man's tasks based on the gender, rather than carefully considering actual individual skill, interest, and availability.

Meanwhile, the man receiving the list may feel obligated to dutifully figure each task out solo due to societal gender norms pressuring capability around home projects as a measure of masculinity. But, in reality, his wife might be better equipped and more interested to efficiently tackle many of the requested projects herself.

Partners also frequently differ in their willingness and threshold to pay for hiring professional help versus taking on projects solo. These disconnects in motivation require open communication to prevent brewing resentment.

Impacts on Relationships

The existence of a lengthy, lingering Honey Do list filled with unfinished home repairs, maintenance, and improvement projects can exert significant detrimental impacts on the happiness, satisfaction, and stability of romantic relationships over time.

Several key factors contribute to how these ubiquitous lists can foster disconnect and discontent between partners. Read on.

Unfinished Projects Undermine Trust

- Incomplete or low-quality workmanship on projects assigned to a partner undermines confidence and satisfaction in the relationship.
- The partner requesting work feels frustrated by lack of tangible progress, while the assignee feels nagged.

Prioritization Disagreements

- Partners frequently disagree over how to prioritize the requested tasks in terms of sequence and importance (HomeTun, 2023).
- One partner may see certain projects as urgent, while the other considers them discretionary upgrades. This difference in viewpoints leads to conflicts.

Unfair Generalizations Based on Gender

- Making DIY assignments based predominantly on gender rather than actual individual interest or ability tends to exacerbate tensions (Liu, 2023).
- Each partner likely possesses certain maintenance, upgrade, and repair skills based on experience, not strictly gender. But assumptions persist.
- Assuming home projects fall exclusively on the man ignores this reality and builds resentment.

Financial Stress

- Underlying money factors also commonly lead to conflicts over Honey Do lists between spouses.
- Partners may disagree on budgeting for hiring professionals versus investing significant DIY time and effort.
- Unexpected costs and complications mid project also frequently generate arguments and dissatisfaction.

Detrimental Impacts on Relationship Health

The scenario of one partner persistently nagging the other over unfinished Honey Do list items can be highly detrimental to overall relationship health and stability over time for the following reasons:

- The ongoing sense of frustration, aggravation, and arguments generated by these lists negatively impacts marital satisfaction.
- Perpetual disappointment in a partner's lack of follow-through also erodes trust and contentment within the partnership.

Without proper communication and collaboration, the Honey Do list phenomenon too often leads to disconnect and discord between couples, undermining the sense of shared teamwork and goals so essential for thriving, long-term relationships.

Rethinking the Honey Do List

While the Honey Do list has developed a notorious reputation for generating frustration and relationship conflicts, the key to remedying these issues is to thoughtfully rethink the very way couples approach this ubiquitous cultural phenomenon.

With the establishment of proper frameworks, open communication channels, and a spirit of collaboration, the dreaded Honey Do list can evolve into a shared tool for accomplishing meaningful goals, deepening intimacy, and creating pride in your living space together. This cultural trope can transform from notorious burden into productive opportunity.

It starts with partners cultivating a habit of open, candid, nonjudgmental communication regarding each other's genuine abilities, interests, motivations, and reservations when it comes to home repairs and improvements. Dangerous assumptions should not be made about who will take responsibility for which tasks on the list. Both individuals need to honestly discuss and assess actual skills, willingness, available time, and thresholds for outsourcing professional help (Liu, 2023).

Making DIY assignments and delegations based predominantly on actual individual skill sets, experience levels, and interests rather than outdated gender stereotypes and roles is also crucial for improving the Honey Do list dynamic (Handyman, 2023). Partners should thoughtfully talk through each requested project first to mutually determine who makes the most sense to take ownership of it based on factors like past experience— not prescribed societal gender norms.

Cultivating an overall spirit of enthusiastic collaboration around the list rather than just delegation can significantly improve the tone, process, and outcome. Both partners should actively contribute ideas for projects based on their own priorities. And each person can provide hands-on assistance, encouragement, and accountability on tasks, regardless of who takes the lead. Approach projects together like gathering materials as a team, providing an extra set of hands when useful, and calling in professional help when warranted (My Creative Days, 2023).

Finally, a powerful way for couples to improve their Honey Do list dynamic while strengthening their relationship is to purposely build shared confidence, skills, and interest in DIY repairs and projects together as an intimate, bonding experience. Take a home improvement course together, watch online tutorial videos as a couple, and start small by doing introductory projects side-by-side. Investing in this foundation enables you to rely less frequently on outside contractors, while enjoying wins through shared effort (Liu, 2023).

With the right frameworks, mindsets, and communication practices in place, the notorious Honey Do list can transform from relationship liability to rewarding collaboration opportunity.

CASE STUDY

Dan and Mindy were eager to put their personal touches on their new home, a charming but outdated, 1930s bungalow. Mindy immediately began pinning decor ideas on Pinterest for

DIY projects to modernize each room. Her digital inspiration board quickly led to a handwritten Honey Do list on the fridge, assigning tasks to Dan.

Dan felt anxious looking at the growing list. "My dad never did home repairs, so I didn't learn basics like using tools or fixing things. Seeing all these projects made me feel inadequate," Dan admitted.

Over time, tension escalated. Mindy felt frustrated by the lack of progress, while Dan grew resentful of projects he lacked the skills for.

Finally, the couple decided to learn DIY skills together. They did online research, watched tutorials, and invested in starter toolkits. Weekend tasks became opportunities to bond while enhancing their home. A year later, Dan's sense of accomplishment continues to grow with each completed project.

The Emotional Labor Imbalance

The partner who creates the list takes on the mental load and emotional labor of not just identifying needs, but also remembering and managing the tasks. The other partner's role becomes limited to just physical execution. This disconnect can brew resentment on both sides over time.

Unreasonable Workload Expectations

In their enthusiasm, the task assigner often overloads the list with nonurgent beautification projects and upgrades that feel like burdensome "honey-do's" not "want-to-do's" to the recipient. This overwhelms the partner and sets them up for failure.

Gender Stereotypes and Norms

Outdated societal gender stereotypes also fuel the cycle, with home maintenance and repairs still primarily perceived as masculine duties. This adds pressure on men to take on laborious unwanted tasks out of shame, while dissuading their female partners from proactively developing useful DIY skills.

Conflict Avoidance

Recipients often passively accept overflowing Honey Do lists to avoid disappointing their eager spouse or appearing lazy, even when feeling overwhelmed and disinterested. This breeds covert resentment over time.

Poor Communication and Collaboration

Lack of clear communication, inefficient delegation of tasks based on interest, not gender, and minimal collaboration lead to disorder. Recipients feel singled out as solely responsible, when homes require teamwork.

The Solution: Rethinking the Honey Do List

The key to turning the Honey Do list from a dreaded source of angst into a productive tool for accomplishing mutually desired home upgrades lies in rethinking the current flawed approach.

With improved communication, proper collaboration, and a spirit of working together, couples can transform the way they distribute home tasks. Here are some tips:

- **Set realistic expectations.** Don't overload one partner. Determine priorities together.
- **Discuss interests and skills.** Assign tasks based on ability, not gender.
- **Collaborate.** Offer to help gather materials and provide hands-on assistance.
- **Communicate concerns.** Agree on a reasonable timeline and budget.
- **Share responsibility.** Take turns adding items important to each of you.
- **Learn skills together.** Attend workshops as a couple. Tackle projects as a team.
- **Celebrate wins.** Express appreciation for effort and accomplishments.

With the proper approach, the Honey Do list can evolve from an infamous point of contention to a rewarding shared tool for accomplishing mutual home improvement goals and bonding.

THE PSYCHOLOGY BEHIND THE LIST

When examining the persistent cultural phenomenon of the Honey Do list, it is insightful to explore the nuanced psychology and motivations underlying both the partner initially making these domestic requests and the recipient feeling pressured to comply.

Gaining empathy into both perspectives through a psychological lens enables couples to improve communication and recalibrate this common relationship stress point.

Psychology of the Honey Do List Requester

For the partner who creates and delivers the Honey Do list of requested home repairs, upgrades, and other tasks for their significant other, the intentions most often stem from fairly benign, though sometimes misguided, motivations.

Typically, the list creator has a desire to assist in improving and beautifying the home environment; they gently prod their spouse into pitching in and productively contributing through completion of tasks. The act of compiling a Honey Do list can represent a partner's attempt to identify, remember, and capture necessary home maintenance work in addition to new projects that would enhance the space.

In addition, the endless sources of stylish home design ideas on digital platforms like Pinterest, combined with societal pressures to maintain high property values through upgrades, further contribute to the appeal of delegating desired projects and upgrades through a Honey Do list.

However, without proper open communication, collaboration, and context provided upfront, this list of solicited Honey Do's can too easily be interpreted as a set of demanding directives rather than helpful suggestions or reminders. Rarely is adequate background conveyed explaining the underlying motivations or reasons for requesting the various tasks, the desired timeline for completing them, or what level of priority each task holds.

Partners also inherently have very different personal preferences and tolerances for contentedly living with existing home flaws versus zealously driving continual discretionary enhancement projects purely for the sake of enhancement or keeping up appearances. This disconnect in home improvement orientation can influence perceptions of the Honey Do list.

Psychology of the Honey Do List Recipient

For the partner on the receiving end of a lengthy Honey Do list full of requested home repairs, maintenance jobs, and improvement projects, anxiety and feeling overwhelmed often quickly ensues. This is especially common among male recipients who question their own capabilities around DIY tasks and home repairs typically characterized as stereotypically "masculine" duties.

Rather than feeling motivated and inspired when presented with a wide-ranging list of unfamiliar domestic projects, men assigned a series of ambiguous Honey Do's can often feel inadequate, uncertain where to start, and generally resentful of the implied mandate to single-handedly figure it out, nonetheless.

Having home repairs and projects delegated to them rather than being consulted on which particular tasks they are actually interested in taking on also understandably fosters resentment and avoidance behaviors in the recipient partner.

Faced with a lengthy list of DIY home projects that range from the mundane, like cleaning rain gutters, to the complex, like electrical repairs, engenders stress and self-doubt, especially among those lacking baseline competence, time, and confidence in home maintenance skills. No one likes to feel set up for failure.

While the Honey Do list originator's motivations are typically benign, if misguided, the recipient partner often feels anxious, overwhelmed, and unduly pressured. This reveals a psychological disconnect that improved communication, empathy, collaboration and realistic expectations can help remedy.

Suggestions for Improving the Honey Do List Dynamic

- Set reasonable project timelines accounting for existing commitments.
- Explain reasons and priorities for requested tasks.
- Consult partner's interests before delegating responsibilities.
- Ask how you can provide support as a team.
- Schedule project status check-ins to show initiative.
- Express appreciation for completed tasks, no matter how small.
- Don't let requests turn into perceived nagging.

With understanding and adjusting the flawed psychology perpetuating problematic Honey Do list dynamics, couples can reframe the experience as a collaborative partnership for bettering their home life together.

THE IMPACT ON RELATIONSHIPS

The existence of a lengthy, lingering Honey Do list filled with unfinished home repairs, maintenance, and improvement projects can exert significant detrimental impacts on the health, happiness, and stability of romantic relationships over time.

Several key factors contribute to how these ubiquitous lists can foster disconnect and discontent between partners.

Unfinished Tasks Undermine Trust

- Incomplete or low-quality workmanship on projects assigned to a partner undermines confidence and satisfaction in the relationship.
- The partner requesting work feels frustrated and nagged by the lack of tangible progress, while the assignee feels micromanaged.

Ongoing Disagreements

- Partners frequently argue over how to prioritize the requested tasks, who should take responsibility for what, and timelines.
- There are often differences in opinion on the necessity or value of requested projects.

- This ongoing contention creates resentment on both sides over time.

Unfair Generalizations Based on Gender

- Making DIY assignments predominantly based on gender rather than actual skills and interest tends to exacerbate tensions.
- Assumptions are made that the man should handle certain repairs based on stereotypes.
- Partners are not evaluated objectively on abilities, only outdated norms.

Financial Stress

- Underlying financial disagreements over budgets lead to conflicts about hiring contractors versus DIY labor.
- Partners argue over taking on debt for home improvements versus living with existing conditions.

Erosion of Partnership

- According to psychologist Bella DePaulo, the scenario of one partner persistently nagging the other over delayed Honey Do projects predicts lower marital stability and satisfaction over time (DePaulo, 2022).
- Ongoing disappointment in a partner's lack of follow-through also degrades trust and contentment.

Suggested Improvements

- Set realistic timelines accounting for other commitments.
- Reassign tasks based on skills, not gender assumptions.
- Compromise on project necessity and cost concerns.
- Schedule periodic progress reviews to prompt momentum.
- Offer to hire help for more complex tasks.
- Show appreciation for all efforts, big and small.

With mutual understanding and a spirit of working together, the Honey Do list can be transformed from a relationship liability into an opportunity for shared growth through home improvements.

KEYS TO SUCCESS

While the infamous Honey Do list has rightfully earned a reputation as a major source of relationship stress and discord, the key to turning this problematic dynamic around is to reframe the very concept of the Honey Do list itself.

With the establishment of proper frameworks, open communication channels, and a spirit of mutual support, couples can transform the Honey Do list from a dreaded source of nagging and arguments into a shared tool for accomplishing meaningful goals, deepening intimacy, and creating pride in your home.

This begins with partners cultivating the perspective of the Honey Do list as an opportunity to work together to upgrade their living space, not a one-sided set of demands. The list becomes symbolic of your shared journey rather than a wedge between spouses.

Next are some key tips to guide this relationship-enriching reframing of the Honey Do process.

Foster Open Communication

- Have candid discussions about motivations, timelines, and priorities for requested projects.
- Explain reasons tasks are important to you and consult your partner's opinions.
- Maintain an ongoing open dialogue to incorporating feedback.

Play to Individual Strengths

- Make assignments based on skills and interests, not gender assumptions.
- Acknowledge there are tasks each partner will be more capable at and enthusiastic about.
- Regularly exchange thoughts on how to best divide and conquer projects.

Cultivate a Spirit of Collaboration

- Approach projects together with both partners contributing ideas, energy, and talents.
- Rather than delegating tasks, use inclusive language like "let's" complete this project.
- Maintain consistent enthusiasm and encouragement, even during challenging stages.

Celebrate Shared Wins

- Make a point to celebrate milestone completions together before moving on to the next project.
- Express sincere gratitude and appreciation for your partner's efforts.
- Let accomplishing projects strengthen your bond and confidence as a couple.

Reframe the Honey Do list as an opportunity to collaborate, gain skills together, and enrich your relationship and living space. With teamwork, appreciation, and open communication, it can evolve into a rewarding shared journey.

Other Tips for Success

- Set realistic timelines that account for other commitments.
- Check in regularly on progress.
- Reprioritize tasks if situations change.

- Offer hands-on help when possible.
- Rely on each partner's strengths.
- Be willing to hire help when needed.
- Maintain patience during setbacks.
- Focus on safety and quality over speed.
- Infuse humor and positivity into the process.
- Celebrate small wins along the way.

With the proper motivations, frameworks, and communication habits, tackling home projects becomes an arena for greater connection, intimacy, fulfillment, and pride that permeates a relationship at its core.

Now that we have explored the complex psychology and dynamics behind the Honey Do list, let's dive into some strategies for cultivating DIY skills and confidence to start methodically tackling those lingering home projects.

Building Confidence in DIY

Completing do-it-yourself (DIY) and home improvement projects requires more than just tools and materials—it also requires confidence. Shockingly, studies have shown that up to 85% of men report lacking the confidence to tackle basic home repairs and maintenance (Family Handyman, 2023). This DIY skills gap and accompanying self-doubt helps explain why those Honey Do lists remain perpetually unfinished.

The psychological impacts of avoiding DIY extend far beyond just incomplete projects around the house. Research has demonstrated that successfully taking on home repairs and improvements builds greater self-esteem and instills an enhanced sense of competence and independence (Bob Vila, 2021). Being able to contribute to your home environment and care for your living space fosters confidence and purpose.

UNDERSTANDING THE PSYCHOLOGY BEHIND DIY

Delving deeper into the psychology behind why taking on DIY and home improvement projects can be so incredibly rewarding and empowering reveals some fascinating insights.

Much of the satisfaction and meaning we gain from successfully completing DIY and maintenance tasks around our home stems from such projects fulfilling a number of core underlying human psychological needs, as described next.

Fulfilling the Need for Competence

Learning new hands-on skills and subsequently achieving the desired fix or upgrade outcomes boosts feelings of self-confidence and capability. Likewise, overcoming initial self-doubt to acquire DIY competency through practice is hugely empowering.

Satisfying the Need for Autonomy

Exerting control over your living environment by customizing and upgrading based on your own visions and choices meets a deep need for independence and self-determination.

Strengthening Relatedness

Improving your home life through projects ultimately strengthens family and community relationships and bonds by virtue of creating a better shared living space.

Boosting Self-Esteem and Meaning

Providing a well-kept home for your family and successfully completing home repairs generates immense pride, purpose, and meaning.

Enabling Creative Outlets

DIY provides a highly constructive outlet for creativity and self-expression. The ability to mold your personal living space based on your own style provides great personal satisfaction.

Additional Psychological Benefits

Various studies have shown that the hands-on learning process involved in DIY projects stimulates the brain, improves focus and concentration, enhances visuospatial and mathematical abilities, and strengthens overall problem-solving skills.

The measurable cognitive benefits of DIY include increased blood flow and connections forming between neurons in the areas of the brain that control memory, learning, and emotion regulation.

Additionally, the huge sense of accomplishment that comes from successfully figuring out and completing DIY repairs and upgrades mostly or entirely on your own, rather than always paying professionals, does wonders for self-assurance and resilience.

While many may initially lack confidence in their DIY skills, pushing past that self-doubt and persevering to acquire handy abilities brings tremendous pride.

Psychologically speaking, DIY projects uniquely satisfy core self-actualization needs, boost cognitive functioning, provide creative outlets, build self-esteem, and deliver an empowering sense of independence and control over your living space. This helps explain why, for many, DIY has become such a rewarding and therapeutic hobby.

HOW DIY BUILDS CONFIDENCE

Statistics reveal that many men lack confidence when it comes to DIY capabilities despite a long-standing cultural assumption that household repairs and projects fall within their domain.

This self-doubt stems in part from an outdated—yet lingering—stigma that men should inherently possess technical know-how around the home, leaving some afraid to admit they need to learn these skills just like anyone else. The reality is that DIY knowledge comes from education and experience, not gender. No one is simply born an expert.

When faced with lengthy Honey Do lists loaded with unfamiliar projects, it's understandable that apprehension creeps in for the uninitiated. But avoidance only breeds more performance anxiety. Putting in time developing core competency around home repairs and improvements builds the assurance needed to successfully cross off tasks.

The psychological impacts of shying away from DIY due to uncertainty or lack of knowledge go beyond the unfinished projects themselves. Avoidance can damage self-confidence and create tension within relationships. But taking the initiative to learn needed skills counteracts these detrimental effects.

Studies show that cultivating DIY skills at any age enhances self-esteem, instills feelings of competency and independence, reduces stress through creative flow, and strengthens self-reliance (Cave, 2019). Investing yourself in the betterment of your home also generates an immense sense of purpose and pride.

QUICK TIPS FOR BUILDING DIY CONFIDENCE

Luckily, developing greater DIY confidence is within reach for anyone willing to put in the time gaining foundational skills. By learning a few basic techniques, taking advantage of available resources, and starting small with simple projects, even the most uncertain novice can safely and successfully begin building know-how.

Here are some quick tips for how to start cultivating DIY confidence:

- **Start small.** Don't overextend yourself early on. Build skills gradually beginning with easy tasks before attempting more difficult projects.
- **Learn the basics.** Get comfortable with essential skills like measuring, cutting, drilling, sanding, leveling, and so on.
- **Use online resources.** From YouTube tutorials to home improvement websites, take advantage of the wealth of guidance available.
- **Invest in tools.** Having the proper tools makes any DIY project easier and more enjoyable.
- **Create a workspace.** Set up an organized work area to comfortably practice fundamental skills.
- **Enlist help.** Don't be afraid to call in skilled friends or family for coaching.
- **Remember safety first.** Never skimp on safety gear and know when to call in a professional.
- **Start with repairs.** Maintaining and fixing things around the house builds practical know-how.
- **Be patient.** Remember that skills take time and practice to develop. Don't get frustrated.
- **Make it fun.** Adding an element of fun will make DIY rewarding, instead of a dreaded chore.

By embracing DIY as a lifelong journey of learning rather than seeking instant perfection, anyone can gain the fundamental skills and confidence needed to successfully take on projects like a seasoned pro. Passion will grow organically through small wins.

CASE STUDY: A FIRST-TIMER'S PATH TO DIY CONFIDENCE

Rick had always shied away from anything related to home maintenance or repairs. He was the first to admit he was not "the handy type." Any time something broke or needed an upgrade around the house, Rick was quick to call a professional rather than attempting the work himself.

But as these service calls became more frequent after purchasing an older home, Rick grew tired of spending so much just to hang a picture or install a new appliance.

"I was pretty much useless when it came to anything DIY. I had no experience and lacked the confidence to even try," Rick admitted.

After a lengthy Honey Do list from his wife, Kelly, included some seemingly simple projects, Rick decided it was time to learn basic home maintenance skills for the sake of their budget—and his pride.

He started small by watching online tutorials focused on fundamentals like using hand tools, drilling holes, patching drywall, and wood sanding. After practicing on scrap materials, Rick successfully installed a new bathroom faucet and fixed some minor drywall damage.

Each project he completed gave Rick more assurance to take on the next repair. Over time, his motivation grew from just saving money on service calls to actually enjoying the process of nurturing his home improvement skills.

A year later, Rick can now comfortably tackle minor electrical work, plumbing repairs, cabinet installations, and more—all tasks that once induced major anxiety.

"Looking back, I can't believe I used to be so intimidated by DIY projects," said Rick. "By starting small and being patient as my skills developed, I've gained the confidence to take care of our home myself."

IMPORTANCE OF PROPER TOOLS

Now that we've covered the psychological boost DIY can provide, having the proper tools is essential for safely and effectively completing projects with precision. Investing in quality tools not only saves money over time, but also makes the process more efficient and enjoyable.

Proper tools act as an extension of your hands, allowing you to exert force and manipulate materials in ways human hands cannot on their own. For example, a hammer provides concentrated striking force, pliers provide gripping strength, and a saw cuts with precision.

Having the right tools for the task also minimizes safety risks. Using the wrong tool in an unsafe manner can lead to slip-ups and injuries. Investing in quality tools designed for the specific job leads to accurate and safe results.

In addition, proper tools allow jobs to be completed faster and with significantly less effort on your part. Trying to turn a screw into wood with just your fingers would be extremely difficult. But using a power drill with the right bit allows for quick progress. The right tools reduce frustration and make the experience more rewarding.

Tools also improve the final product's quality and longevity. Cutting wood precisely to length with a miter saw ensures proper fit and function compared to crude, uneven hand cuts. And fastening materials together with the recommended screws or nails guarantees stability and strength.

Having tools immediately available when needed also improves efficiency by minimizing downtime searching for a missing item. An organized toolbox, pegboard, or shelving system in your workspace keeps tools securely stowed, yet accessible.

While quality tools represent an upfront investment, the expense pays off significantly over time. Well-made tools last for years when properly cared for. A robust set of essentials such as a drill, saw, wrenches, clamps, and more will equip you for a wide range of DIY projects.

When starting out, don't feel compelled to purchase every tool right away. Start with versatile basics like hammers, screwdrivers, pliers, and wrenches. Add to your collection over time as your skills progress. And you may find certain specialty tools are better to rent or borrow rather than own.

With the right set of tools, along with proper guidance, you can gain skills, confidence, and satisfaction advancing from DIY novice to seasoned expert. Your toolset will grow with you as you conquer ever more complex home improvement projects.

While home improvement projects may seem daunting, developing fundamental DIY skills can transform uncertainty into confidence. Strengthening your capabilities and know-how around basic repairs and enhancements helps get things done while also cultivating self-assurance. Yet statistics reveal a persistent skills gap when it comes to men's comfort level with household projects.

This uncertainty damages self-esteem when faced with lengthy Honey Do lists. But the good news is that building core competency around home improvements is achievable for anyone willing to put in the time developing foundational skills.

Beyond the practical impact, successfully taking on home repairs and upgrades builds greater self-confidence and instills an enhanced sense of competence and independence (Mosier, 2021). Being able to care for your living environment and contribute to your home fosters self-reliance and purpose.

Hands-on learning stimulates the brain, improves focus, and enhances problem-solving abilities according to studies (Cave, 2019). DIY provides a constructive outlet for creativity. Pride and satisfaction come from skill mastery.

When starting out, focus on fundamentals like measuring, cutting, drilling, sanding, and leveling. Learn the capabilities and proper use of essential tools. Start with easy fixes and upgrades before attempting more difficult projects.

Patience is key—skills develop over time and through practice. Follow tutorials, enlist guidance from experienced friends, and don't get frustrated. With a step-by-step approach, even DIY novices can gain lifelong skills to take on a wide range of improvements.

Equipped with enhanced confidence and capability, it's essential we build up the right tools for successfully completing common home repairs and upgrades over time.

Tools of the Trade

Having the proper tools on hand is essential for completing DIY and home improvement projects efficiently and with quality results. The right tools allow you to tackle a wide range of repairs, installations, maintenance, and upgrades around the home (This Old House, 2010). As your experience grows over time, gradually build up a comprehensive toolkit tailored to the types of projects you take on.

Invest in the highest-quality tools you can comfortably afford, which will pay off significantly over years of use on projects. Maintain tools properly, inspecting for damage periodically. Add specialty tools over time as your capabilities grow. With the right fundamental toolkit, you'll gain confidence to handle common DIY tasks around the home.

ESSENTIAL TOOLS FOR DIY SUCCESS

Tom was eager to take on his first big DIY project—installing a new bathroom vanity. After watching a few YouTube tutorials, he felt ready. Tom drove to the home improvement store, loaded up his car with the new vanity, and rushed back home, tools in hand.

As he unpacked everything, Tom suddenly realized he was missing a key tool—a drill. Without it, he had no way to attach the vanity to the wall or install the faucet. An hour later, after returning from the store to purchase a drill, Tom finally got to work.

After struggling to assemble the new vanity with just a screwdriver, Tom was frustrated. This experience made him realize the importance of having the proper tools for the job.

Having a fully stocked toolbox is one of the keys to DIY success. The right tools allow you to work quickly, efficiently, and safely on home projects. Investing in quality tools will also save you money over hiring others for repairs and improvements.

Learning how to properly use tools takes time and practice. Always review manuals and safety procedures. Don't overestimate your skills and attempt unsafe operations. Start with small projects to build experience.

With the right tools and knowledge, you'll gain the skills you need to take on a wide range of DIY tasks with precision and confidence.

MUST-HAVE POWER TOOLS

Power tools utilize electricity (either corded or battery powered) to accomplish tasks with greater speed, accuracy, and efficiency than could reasonably be achieved using just manual hand tools and human muscle power alone. Having a selection of both power tools and non-powered hand tools in your arsenal provides the versatility to tackle the widest range of DIY projects.

Some of the most essential power tools to invest in for home improvement projects are described next.

Cordless Drill

A cordless drill provides portable rotary power perfect for drilling holes and driving screws. Look for one with adjustable torque and variable speed settings to match the needs of different materials and tasks. A drill with a keyed chuck also allows you to quickly change between drill bits and screw-driving heads. A versatile cordless drill is one of the most frequently used power tools for DIYers.

Circular Saw

A circular saw (corded or cordless) is ideal for accurately cutting lumber, plywood, trim, flooring and more to length during projects. Choose a model that allows adjustments to the cut depth and offers the ability to angle the blade for angled cuts. A guide track improves cutting straight lines. An indispensable tool for accurate straight line cutting.

Jigsaw

A jigsaw enables you to cut curved lines and openings in wood, laminate, countertops, drywall, and other materials where a circular saw blade won't fit. The thin reciprocating blade allows tightly maneuvering corners. It's extremely useful for cutting custom openings in countertops, cabinets, and walls. An orbiter feature further improves cutting curves.

Random Orbital Sander

A random orbital sander is ideal for smoothing and removing material from wood while preparing surfaces for finishing. The random sanding motion adapts well to contours and prevents leaving swirl marks. Consider models that allow hooking up a shop vac for dust collection. Maintain a selection of coarse to fine grit sandpaper discs.

Cordless Power Screwdriver

Cordless power screwdrivers can rapidly drive screws with more torque and less effort than manual screwdrivers. This greatly speeds up projects that require installing numerous screws like building decks, bookcases, and sheds. Look for lithium-ion models with ergonomic grip design to minimize hand fatigue.

Investing in these core power tools provides the fundamental capabilities to efficiently cut, drill, shape, smooth, and join materials for nearly any home-building or remodeling project. Buy the highest-quality power tools you can reasonably afford, and they'll last for many years, even with frequent heavy use. Start with these essentials and gradually add to your power tool arsenal over time as needs arise.

MUST-HAVE HAND TOOLS

While power tools provide speed and strength, stocking the following key hand tools is equally essential:

- **Hammers:** A 16- or 20-oz claw hammer is extremely versatile for driving and pulling nails, light demolition, and peening. Consider a rubber mallet for delicate work. Always use the proper hammer for the task (Family Handyman, 2023).
- **Screwdrivers:** A set with multiple flathead and Phillips head screwdrivers in a range of sizes suits most tasks. Choose durable alloy steel shafts. Proper size reduces stripping screw heads (This Old House, 2010).
- **Levels:** A larger level for walls and a smaller one for cabinets and shelves to ensure they are even.
- **Handsaw:** A pull saw with a fine-toothed blade to cut trim boards, dowels, and other thin wood.
- **Clamps:** Locking C-clamps to temporarily hold glued boards or objects being nailed or screwed.

- **Socket sets:** Standard and metric socket sets and wrenches for tightening automotive and equipment hardware.
- **Pliers:** Needle-nose, slip joint, groove joint, and tongue-and-groove pliers allow you to firmly grip items. Use to manipulate nuts, bolts, pipes, wires, and more (Family Handyman, 2023).
- **Tape measure:** A 25-foot tape is ideal for taking measurements during projects and layouts. Look for automatic recoil and a finger stop (This Old House, 2010).
- **Utility knife:** Features quick blade changes and a retractable blade to safely score materials for cutting. Use for opening boxes, too (Family Handyman, 2023).
- **Wrenches:** Use box-end, open-end, and adjustable wrenches in standard and metric sizes for assembling and disassembling many items (This Old House, 2010).
- **Safety gear:** Equip your toolbox with safety glasses, work gloves, ear protection, dust masks, and knee pads to prevent injury (Family Handyman, 2023).

Properly-cared-for quality hand tools can serve reliably for a lifetime. Start with this foundation of classic hand tools to handle basic DIY tasks on their own or in conjunction with power tools when needed for heavy tasks.

SAFETY GEAR

Never neglect personal safety—invest in these essentials:

- Safety goggles to shield eyes from flying debris
- Ear protection, such as noise-dampening earmuffs, when using loud power tools
- Dust masks for filtering fine airborne sawdust particles
- Work gloves to protect hands and improve grip on tools
- Steel-toe boots for heavy tasks
- Knee pads to provide cushion when kneeling

Take your time to build up a comprehensive toolkit consisting of well-made hand tools, specialized power tools tailored to common needs, and protective safety gear. This home improvement armory will empower you to take on a limitless range of DIY projects and repairs!

HAND TOOLS FOR PRECISION

While power tools provide the brute repetitive forces and torque needed for cutting, drilling, and driving fasteners into dense materials, hand tools allow for more controlled finessed precision and detail work. Having a quality collection of hand tools ensures you can work accurately, safely and efficiently on the intricacies that power tools aren't well suited for.

Screwdrivers

A comprehensive selection of screwdrivers (both flathead and Phillips head varieties) in a range of sizes is indispensable for driving or removing the many types of screws and fasteners encountered during DIY projects and repairs. Look for corrosion-resistant heat-treated chrome vanadium alloy steel shafts with machined tips that resist wear and damage. Durable molded handles provide grip.

Pliers

Pliers in various styles, such as needle-nose, slip joint, groove joint, and tongue-and-groove, allow firmly grasping, turning, bending, and repositioning nuts, bolts, wires, nails, and other hardware by hand when finesse is required. The adjustable jaws of slip-joint and groove-joint pliers enable custom clamping for different tasks. Use pliers for detailed work like gripping nails to start them or holding tiny hardware pieces in place.

Hammers

A general-purpose 16-ounce curved-claw hammer is extremely versatile for driving and pulling nails, as well as peening and light demolition work. The curved claw is ideal for pulling nails. Consider also getting a rubber- or dead-blow mallet for delicate tapping work where a steel head may damage surfaces. A smaller trim hammer allows driving slim finish nails.

Handsaws

For detailed trim work and cuts in tight spaces, a small backsaw where the blade is reinforced with a stiffening rib is ideal—they cut efficiently on the pull stroke only. Look for razor-sharp hardened teeth that are precision set for clean, accurate cuts in wood and PVC trim boards. Consider both fine- and extra-fine-tooth-count blades for superior cuts.

Wrenches

A range of nonratcheting combination wrenches, open-end wrenches, box-end wrenches, and adjustable wrenches in both standard and metric sizes are regularly used when assembling furniture, fixtures, plumbing connections, and any job involving nuts, bolts, and pipes. The various types of wrenches allow access in different spaces and scenarios. Keep them organized and at hand.

Utility Knife

A retractable utility knife with quick blade changes is indispensable for opening cardboard boxes and scoring drywall, wood, plastic sheets, and other materials prior to snapping them. The retractable blade prevents accidents. Maintain a stock of heavy-duty replacement blades for peak cutting performance.

Tape Measure

A quality 25-foot-long (or longer) steel-tape measure allows for accurately taking measurements, distances, and dimensions during projects and layouts. Look for tape measures with a finger stop and auto-lock feature to maintain readings rather than recoiling during use. Sturdy clips, finger grips, and a belt hook improve durability.

Having a comprehensive, well-organized collection of hand tools for turning, driving, cutting, scraping, measuring, and gripping provides the capability to complete detailed assembly work, fine-trim carpentry, fussy repairs, precision measurements, and other key tasks not easily done with brute-force power tools alone.

Maintain sharp-blade edges on all cutting tools for safety and optimal performance. Keep sliding mechanisms like pliers and wrenches properly lubricated to prevent binding. Replace any heavily worn or damaged hand tools. Properly-cared-for hand tools can provide decades of reliable service. Invest in quality brands and continue expanding your collection as your project skills grow.

Essential Hand Tool Usage Tips

Here are some key tips for effectively utilizing hand tools:

- **Use the right size tool for screws and bolts.** Avoid stripping heads or rounding flats.

- **When sawing, let the blade do the cutting.** Don't force cuts. Long strokes utilize the entire blade.
- **Support what you're working on properly.** Use clamps and vises to prevent shifting.
- **Grip pliers on the knurled section for maximum leverage.** Don't just pinch the tips.
- **Tap gently with a hammer.** A smooth swing gains momentum to strike the blows when needed.
- **Keep the utility knife blade retracted when not in use.** Extend only when actively cutting.
- **Pull tape measures rather than letting them recoil.** This reduces wear and prevents inaccurate readings.

Hand tools may seem basic, but mastering proper selection and usage techniques vastly improves your precision, control, and accuracy on detail DIY work. Combine with power tools as needed to complete ambitious projects from start to finish.

Safety Note: Always wear protective eyewear when using hand tools. Take care to protect your hands from sharp tools and flying debris.

TOOL STORAGE AND ORGANIZATION

As your collection of tools and supplies grows over time with increased DIY experience, properly storing everything neatly and systematically keeps your inventory easily accessible yet secure. Well-organized tools also minimize risk of damage. Cluttered tools lead to frustration.

Consider some tips for effectively storing tools and hardware, as shown next.

Wall-Mounted Storage

- Pegboards with customizable hooks allow tracing tool outlines to create custom organized storage.
- Wall-mounted cabinets with doors keep dangerous tools like saws safely locked away while close at hand.
- Shelving units work for holding bulkier items. Sturdy brackets and bracing provide support.
- Wall control panels have specialty holders for everything from gardening tools to paint rollers.

Portable Storage

- A high-quality rolling toolbox or work cart provides portable access to your most-used tools anywhere around the house.
- Clear plastic tackle boxes, parts cases, and small-parts organizers allow sorting and transporting hardware like screws, nails, nuts, bolts, washers, and more. Label the lids for quick identification.
- Metal or heavy-duty plastic toolboxes come in stacks or as rolling chests. They provide multiple drawers, trays, and storage compartments specialized for securely holding tools.

Floor Storage

- Waterproof utility storage totes keep categorized supplies for specific projects together. Label the lids clearly.
- Hanging racks safely store long tools like rakes, shovels, and broom handles at an angle for access.
- Sturdy fixed-height or rolling workbenches provide ample flat space for active project work using bench-top tools. Add drawers or shelves for storage underneath.
- Look for heavy-duty cabinets like welding cabinets for protecting expensive power tools when not in use.

General Tips

- Create designated storage zones in the garage, shed, basement, or workshop for different tool categories.
- Store tools close to point of use, when possible— wherever you happen to be working.
- Keep a "necessity zone" tray with your most frequently used tools always conveniently accessible near your workspace.
- Check your inventory before additional tool purchases to avoid duplicate items.
- Consider storing basic tools needed for quick fixes in a portable bag that can be easily carried around the house.

- Maintain an up-to-date written list of all tools for insurance purposes in the event of theft or loss.

No matter the specific approach, having tools and supplies systematically stored reduces time wasted searching for that misplaced drill bit or loose scissors. Organization is the key to efficiency.

Additional Hardware Storage Tips

Properly storing small hardware helps avoid losing pieces. Try these tips:

- Use clear plastic compartment boxes to sort nails, screws, nuts, bolts, and so on.
- Sort hardware on shelves or in drawers by type and size. Label everything clearly.
- Save jars or food containers to hold loose items like washers and nails.
- Keep hardware needed for specific upcoming projects together in resealable bags.
- Never store hazardous chemical containers with (or near) consumables like food.

Take time to continually refine your tool organization methods. Proper storage protects your investments while allowing you to work smoothly and efficiently. Never underestimate the value of tidiness!

TOOL STORAGE ON A BUDGET

Outfitting your DIY workspace with proper storage to keep tools and materials organized certainly doesn't need to cost a fortune. With some creativity and resourcefulness, there are many budget-friendly solutions for creating an efficient space to work.

Listed next are some cost-effective tool storage and organization options to consider when equipping a garage, basement, shed, or workspace on a tight budget.

Pegboard With Custom Outlines: $30

Pegboards allow creating customized tool storage layouts specific to your frequently used items. For around $30 you can get a 4×8-foot pegboard panel and package of hooks. Use a marker to trace outlines of your most-used tools before mounting at a comfortable working height. Custom fitted holes with hooks keep essential items right at hand when needed.

Plastic Organizer Bins: $1–$5 Each

Clear plastic multicompartment organizer bins are extremely useful for sorting small parts like screws, nails, nuts, bolts, washers, etc., by type and size. They cost as little as $1–$5 each. Labelling the lids makes finding the right hardware quick and easy. They can sit on shelves or stack together.

Metal Storage Cabinet: $100

A freestanding, lockable 30–36-inch-wide metal storage cabinet with adjustable shelves provides a secure place to organize hand- and power tools, while protecting them from moisture. Look for used cabinets for around $100. Sturdy wall-mounted metal cabinets are another option.

Concrete Blocks and Boards: $30 Total

An inexpensive sturdy workbench or shelf can be constructed from concrete cinder blocks with plywood or 2×12 boards laid across the top. All materials cost around $30 total. Customize dimensions as needed. Bolt boards together for stability. The open blocks allow storage space below.

Repurposed Dresser: 0–$50

Repurposing an old dresser picked up secondhand or found discarded on bulk garbage day is a characterful way to gain multiple storage drawers and compartments for tools and small parts. Look for sturdy solid-wood examples costing 0–$50. Remove any drawers needing repair.

Other Budget Options

- Shelving units made of 2×4s and plywood
- Repurposed kitchen cabinets for protected storage
- Used commercial wire shelving units

- Salvaged wooden crates and boxes
- 5-gallon buckets for bulk items
- Coffee cans or jars for organizing hardware

The goal is to keep your most frequently used tools directly at hand above all else. For rarely used specialty items, a less convenient storage location works just fine. Gradually improving organization over time naturally leads to a smoother workflow. You don't have to break the bank to get there.

General Affordability Tips

- Check secondhand stores, garage sales, and online classifieds for deals.
- Buy toolbox organizer inserts to customize inexpensive toolboxes.
- Use scrap plywood and 2×4's for building projects.
- Repurpose items from around the house creatively.
- Start with a small workspace and expand over time.

You can create an incredibly functional shop space for under $150 by utilizing pegboards, repurposed furniture, plastic bins, concrete blocks, and other recycled or dollar store–type items. Don't underestimate the power of creativity and resourcefulness for maximizing value.

BUILDING YOUR ARSENAL OVER TIME

When just getting started with home improvement projects, there's no need to feel compelled to purchase every conceivable tool all at once. Begin by investing in a set of rugged, versatile basic hand tools like pliers, screwdrivers, a quality claw hammer, adjustable wrenches, utility knife, tape measure, and safety gear.

Learn proper techniques for using these essential tools effectively by practicing on simpler introductory DIY projects. Allow your arsenal to gradually expand organically as specific needs arise over time. Consider renting or borrowing more specialized tools to help provide insight into which models best suit your unique projects before purchasing.

When making tool purchases, try to buy the highest quality and durability you can reasonably afford, as this pays dividends over the long haul. Building a comprehensive toolkit is a lifelong endeavor. Let your collection grow wisely in step with the evolution of your skills and project experience over the years. Avoid impulse purchases of niche tools that will rarely get used. With proper care and maintenance, many tools can provide decades of reliable service.

While hand-tool technology changes very little over time, do try to invest in the latest lithium-ion battery–powered cordless tools when you upgrade to power tools. Compared to older NiCd batteries, lithium-ion offers extended sustained runtime and more power in a lighter package. Brushless motors increase efficiency and runtime even further in drills, saws, and others.

Take advantage of design improvements that add useful features like built-in LED work lights.

Keep in mind that no prepackaged toolkit available at a big box store contains every single tool needed to complete all tasks and projects. It's best to thoughtfully personalize your toolkit based on the specific types of DIY and repair projects you plan to take on. Then continue refining your arsenal gradually as your experience level and needs evolve organically over your home improvement journey.

Starter Tool Recommendations

Here are some recommended starter tools to get going with common tasks and repairs:

- Claw hammer
- Flat pry bar
- Screwdriver set
- Adjustable wrench set
- Slip-joint pliers
- Utility knife
- Tape measure
- Safety glasses
- Work gloves

After mastering the basics, adding tools from these categories greatly expands your capabilities:

Power Drills and Drivers

- **Cordless drill/driver combo kit:** for drilling and driving screws
- **Impact driver:** provides torque for driving larger fasteners
- **Right-angle drill:** access tight spaces

Saws

- **Circular saw:** cutting boards, plywood, trims to length
- **Jigsaw:** curved cuts and openings
- **Hacksaw:** cutting metal rods, pipes, and more

Wrenches

- **Socket set with ratchet:** for nuts and bolts
- **Allen wrench sets:** metric and standard sizes
- **Open-end/box-end wrench:** for tighter and hard-to-reach areas

Other Essentials

- Clamps
- Chisels
- Pry bar set
- Putty knives
- Files
- Sandpaper

Take inventory of current possessions before making purchases. For example, thoroughly check any old family toolboxes for hidden gems. Review craigslist and thrift stores for quality used tools. Building your capabilities over years through strategic purchases ensures you remain well equipped for projects as they arise while avoiding wasting money on unnecessary tools.

CASE STUDY

James and his wife, Lily, had recently purchased an outdated, but charming, older home. After moving in, Lily began compiling a long list of renovation projects she hoped James could take on, like replacing all the light fixtures, installing new flooring, and painting each room.

Although eager to update their new home, James felt anxious looking at the extensive Honey Do list. He had very little DIY experience.

Lily's grandfather offered James some advice. He explained that having proper tools was key to completing projects efficiently and safely. He gave James a toolbox filled with essentials like a drill, circular saw, wrenches, clamps, and more.

With his new tools, James practiced on small repairs to gain skills and confidence. One Saturday, he decided he was ready to tackle a big project—refinishing their hardwood floors. Thanks to YouTube tutorials and the right tools, it went smoothly.

The more projects James completed around the house, the more his tool collection grew. He also learned how to use each one properly through experience. A year later, Lily remarked at how equipped James was to handle any home repair situation.

Having the proper tools is crucial to DIY success. The right equipment allows you to complete projects efficiently, safely, and with precision. Investing in quality tools also saves money over constantly hiring professionals.

Power tools provide the brute force to get big jobs done. A drill/driver and circular saw should be in every homeowner's arsenal, according to experts (This Old House, 2010). Choose versions with variable speed triggers for control.

For precision work, hand tools are essential. A comprehensive screwdriver set, wrench set, pliers, hammer, utility knife, tape measure, and clamps enable detailed assembly and finishing work (Family Handyman, 2023). Other DIY must-haves include levels, pry bars, ratchets, sandpaper, and caulk guns.

Safety gear like eye protection, dust masks, ear protection, and gloves prevent injuries.

Tool storage keeps your collection organized and damage free. Wall-mounted pegboards, rolling carts, toolboxes, and cabinets all work. Outline shapes on pegboards for fast identification.

Build your toolkit gradually as you gain experience. Focus first on acquiring versatile basics like hammers, screwdrivers, wrenches, and pliers. Add specialty tools later as needed for specific projects.

With research and care, a robust toolset can last decades and provide capabilities for a wide range of DIY projects over your lifetime.

With a robust DIY toolkit in hand, creating an actionable plan for prioritizing and scheduling home improvement projects is crucial for efficiently working through tasks together.

Prioritizing Projects for Success

Between repairs that unexpectedly pop up and exciting new upgrade ideas, it's easy for your home improvement to-do list to become overwhelming. Without proper prioritization, project momentum stalls. You can regain control through smart strategies for deciding which tasks take precedence over others.

Assess both urgency and importance for each project using a simple matrix. Critical repairs like a leaky pipe or a broken appliance rank highly urgent and important. Meanwhile, beautification projects like painting rooms fall lower (Family Handyman, 2023).

Next, evaluate your available bandwidth in terms of time, energy, and resources. Grouping related tasks makes execution more efficient. Consider which projects require assistance from others or special equipment rentals (This Old House, 2009).

Build consensus with family members to align on priorities and avoid confusion. Make a shared calendar noting project plans. Split large endeavors into distinct milestones to maintain motivation as you check items off (My Creative Days, 2023).

Establish a dedicated monthly budget for home improvement, funneling any windfalls into this allocation. Earmark upcoming large outlays. Save up over time for bigger-ticket projects. Take advantage of seasonal sales on needed supplies (This Old House, 2009).

Learn to just say no to outside opinions on what you "should" take on next. Focus your quality time and money on projects with personal significance, not keeping up with others.

By thoughtfully assessing your unique situation, constraints, and goals, you can pursue a strategic order of tasks that keeps momentum going while fitting your lifestyle. Embrace the satisfaction of checking completed items off your DIY to-do list.

MANAGING THE HONEY DO LIST

When facing a lengthy Honey Do list filled with home repairs, upgrades, maintenance, and other tasks for every room, an important question quickly arises: Where do I even begin?

Prioritizing projects strategically is the key to making steady progress on your list without becoming overwhelmed. With proper planning, thorough preparation, consistent communication, and a systematic approach, you can methodically complete tasks both efficiently and effectively while simultaneously keeping your relationship strong.

Start By Creating a Master List

Gather input from your significant other and make a master list of all home improvement projects needed, both small and large. Capture every task, such as:

- **Repairs:** leaky faucets, broken cabinets, damaged walls
- **Maintenance:** gutter cleaning, fertilizing lawns, sealing decks
- **Upgrades:** remodeling bathrooms, installing floors, painting rooms
- **Enhancements:** landscaping yard, adding accent lighting, mounting TVs

Having a centralized list provides clarity on the full scope of work ahead, while allowing you to break it down into manageable pieces.

Prioritize Intelligently

Next, thoughtfully prioritize tasks based on criteria, such as:

- **Safety hazards:** Address any issues that pose immediate risks first.
- **Damage prevention:** Prevent small issues from escalating into bigger, more expensive problems.

- **Functional necessity:** Focus on projects needed for daily living and convenience.
- **Cost efficiency:** Group similar projects together to optimize workflow.
- **Curb appeal:** Make improvements visible to guests and neighbors.
- **Personal goals:** Select a few meaningful DIY skills you want to develop.

Sequence logically from most pressing needs to nice-to-have upgrades. Balance long-term projects with quick wins to build momentum.

Create an Executable Plan

With prioritized tasks, build a step-by-step execution plan:

- Detail all materials and tools needed for each project.
- Estimate costs and create a budget accounting for incidentals.
- Watch online tutorial videos to understand scope and steps involved.
- Break down larger projects into discrete milestones.
- Schedule projects across coming weeks and months with reasonable time buffers.
- Block off calendar commitments before slotting in work sessions.

An executable project plan mapped to your unique schedule and windows of availability brings the prioritized list to life.

Communicate Frequently and Honestly

Openly communicating throughout the process is vital. Following are some examples:

- Set aligned expectations up front on scope, budget, and timeline.
- Provide frequent progress updates and adjust course as needed.
- Discuss any blockers or issues as soon as they arise.
- Request help when feeling overwhelmed or lacking skills.
- Show appreciation for patience and acknowledge inconveniences.

Frequent honest dialogue coupled with transparency ensures you stay on the same page while confronting challenges as a team.

Work in Stages With Momentum

Maintain focus and momentum by working in concentrated stages, like these:

- Complete one space or project type at a time before moving to the next.
- Limit switching between different tasks to maximize efficiency.
- Build on small early wins to create positive momentum.
- Take breaks between project stages to recover and regroup.
- Celebrate milestones reached along the way.

Steady focused progress with strategic breaks keeps you energized, motivated, and moving forward systematically.

By planning thoroughly, prioritizing intelligently, communicating proactively, and maintaining momentum, you can steadily work through a sizable Honey Do list while strengthening partnership in the process.

FACTORS TO CONSIDER WHEN PRIORITIZING

When facing a lengthy Honey Do list filled with assorted home repairs, upgrades, and enhancements, it can feel overwhelming trying to determine where to even begin. The key to success is taking the time up front to thoughtfully think through several key factors when deciding how best to prioritize projects.

Consider the following elements when determining the ideal sequence for tackling tasks on your list.

Evaluate the Urgency

Carefully think through which repairs or issues simply cannot wait versus nice-to-have upgrades that primarily add aesthetic value. Generally, you want to address any immediate pressing safety concerns first before moving on to discretionary beautification projects (Guthrie, 2023). For example, dealing with a leaky pipe or a faulty electrical system requires urgent attention to prevent catastrophic damage or fire hazards, while painting a room a fresh color is purely optional.

Account for Seasonality

Factor in how the time of year and seasonal weather impacts ideal project timing. Certain home projects naturally make more sense to schedule for spring and summer, when you can work comfortably outdoors and open windows, while delaying tasks better suited for fall or winter. For instance, exterior painting or landscaping is best completed when temperatures are mild, while you want to avoid kicking up dust from interior updates during congested holiday seasons, if possible.

Map Out Dependencies

Take time to break down projects and determine which tasks need to be completed first to reasonably enable other related jobs down the line. Essentially, think through the logical order of operations for how projects build on one another. For example, it's prudent to get new flooring installed and settled first, before moving on to update interior wall-paint colors in a room to match the new floors. Being thoughtful about these dependencies will prevent inefficient back-and-forth.

Balance Time Requirements

When sequencing your list, strive to balance larger projects that will require a significant multi day time investment with smaller one-day weekend-type tasks that you can reasonably complete in under 24 hours. Integrating some quick gratifying wins helps build momentum, while only tackling massive renovations can quickly lead to fatigue and stagnation from the prolonged nature of the work. Don't overload yourself out of the gates—think marathon mentality.

Evaluate Required Skills

Take an honest personal inventory of your current DIY skill level and existing knowledge when realistically assessing which tasks you are equipped to successfully take on right now. Be cautious about prematurely biting off more than you can reasonably chew on advanced intricate projects that are far outside your current experience and comfort zone before you've learned the skills you'll need (Family Handyman, 2023). Building confidence first through a wide range of simpler, approachable DIY tasks will prepare you for greater challenges.

Discuss With Your Partner

Make sure to openly communicate with your spouse or partner to get fully aligned on both the composition of, as well as proposed prioritization for, project responsibilities on the shared Honey Do list. Without having an open discussion and getting on the same page about motivations and goals, execution risks deteriorating into arguments down the line. Talk it through together.

Additional Key Considerations

- **Budget:** Balance costlier and more affordable projects. Factor in both material expenses and areas potentially requiring professional subcontractor outsourcing beyond DIY capabilities.
- **Tools/equipment required:** Assess whether you currently have the necessary tools and equipment on hand for a given project, or if purchases would be required.
- **Houseguest visits:** Accelerating certain projects, such as yard landscaping or added seating capacity, may make sense when company is slated to visit.
- **Fatigue:** Mix in less physically demanding tasks between labor-intensive projects to incorporate active recovery periods for your body.

By carefully thinking through all of these key factors during your project-planning process, you can thoughtfully prioritize and sequence the execution of tasks on your Honey Do list in a strategic fashion. This will set you up for steady measurable progress, ongoing motivation, and successful completion.

CREATING AN EFFECTIVE PROJECT MANAGEMENT PLAN FOR DIY PROJECTS

When you're facing a lengthy Honey Do list filled with assorted home repairs, upgrades, and enhancements, having an organized project management plan and checklist can greatly help streamline tackling multiple improvement projects efficiently.

Follow these tips when creating a centralized project plan to stay on track.

Break Large, Complex Projects Into Smaller Subtasks

For expansive remodeling or renovation projects, break down the sizable initiatives into a series of smaller, more manageable and measurable DIY subtasks. This makes the large undertakings feel less daunting, while allowing you to better monitor progress by checking off incremental achievements along the way.

Assign Due Dates for Each Project or Milestone

Assign due dates for the completion of each discrete home improvement project or major milestone phase within complex initiatives. Having defined deadlines creates accountability to stay on schedule and not let items languish half-finished. This will also build in reasonable flex-time buffers for the unknowns and unplanned events that inevitably will arise.

Catalog Any Specific Tools, Materials, or Parts Needed

Make a detailed note of any specific tools, materials, components, hardware, or parts that you will need to complete each unique task or phase. Then check your current inventory to ensure availability, or make a shopping list for items to purchase ahead of time so everything is on hand when required.

Map Out Prerequisite Steps

Identify any prerequisite DIY jobs that will need to be fully completed first before you can reasonably start on subsequent interdependent tasks. Think through the proper sequential order of operations for projects and watch for potential bottlenecks. Arrange your plan accordingly.

Celebrate Completed Items and Milestones

As you proceed through executing your project plan, take time to celebrate and acknowledge the successful completion of each discrete item or major milestone along the way. Checking progress helps maintain ongoing motivation and forward momentum.

Review and Reassess Priorities

Periodically review the full project plan and reconfirm that task priorities are still aligned, or reassess if any adjustments are necessary based on shifting needs, new budget considerations, seasonal constraints, or altered timelines. Project plans are living documents, so update accordingly.

Additional Project Management Best Practices

- Set progress status for tasks: Not Started, In Progress, Completed.
- Note which tasks require hiring professional help.
- Track all expenses against project budget.
- File receipts, warranties, and product manuals.
- Take photos before, during, and after completion.
- Record any lessons learned or tips for next time.
- Share progress and collaborate with your partner frequently.

By investing time in mapping out a centralized, well-thought-out project plan augmented by detailed Honey Do lists and checklists, you can work through DIY home improvements in a far more systematic fashion. This helps overcome the all-too-common cycle of launching enthusiastically into tasks before fizzling out, leaving unfinished projects accumulating. Consistent planning and tracking fosters accountability, alignment, and timely completion.

Prioritize Home Projects

When constructing your project plan, properly prioritizing the sequence for tackling items is critical to working efficiently. Consider the following factors when assessing project priority:

- **Safety:** Address any urgent repairs that pose risks.
- **Damage prevention:** Fix small issues before they escalate.
- **Functionality:** Focus on necessities over aesthetic-only upgrades.
- **Partner needs:** Agree on priority projects that satisfy you both.
- **Quick wins:** Balance larger and smaller tasks.
- **Seasonality:** Schedule exterior work during warmer months.
- **Skills required:** Build confidence before advanced tasks.
- **Tools/materials:** Assess if items required are already owned.
- **Time and labor:** Mix high-effort projects with easier tasks.

Staying organized, prioritizing intelligently, collaborating with your partner, and diligently tracking progress against your plan enables you to steadily work through a sizable Honey Do list while also strengthening relationships through shared accomplishments.

FOSTERING OPEN COMMUNICATION

In addition to proper project planning and preparation, frequently communicating openly, honestly, and regularly with your spouse or partner is a vital component to successfully tackling home improvement projects together.

Schedule both pre-project discussion sessions as well as periodic progress reviews. These check-in conversations provide meaningful opportunities.

Review the Full Project Checklist and Prioritize Order Together

- Sit down together and review the overall Honey Do list project checklist and proposed prioritization plan in detail before diving into execution.
- This ensures everyone is fully aligned on the scope and sequential order before beginning work.
- Gaining shared clarity up front prevents potential confusion or conflicts later on.

Set Clear Mutual Expectations

- Discuss target deadlines for completing each project or phase to set agreed-upon expectations regarding pacing.
- Confirm responsibilities—who will tackle which specific tasks based on interests and capabilities.

- Align on budget, being open about projected costs, and agreements around hiring specialty contractors versus DIY labor.
- Air any concerns transparently so they can be addressed rather than festering.

Realign on Changing Priorities

- Check in periodically to realign on priorities— whether any adjustments are needed based on shifting needs, changing timelines, new constraints arising, or certain tasks taking longer than expected.
- Remain flexible and agree on logical revisions to keep projects moving forward efficiently.

Provide Encouragement and Appreciation

- Provide frequent encouragement and acknowledge achievements as projects get successfully completed. Express sincere gratitude for your partner's efforts!
- To maintain motivation, celebrate milestone victories before moving on to the next phase.

Proper upfront planning and preparation prevents feeling overwhelmed when initially faced with a lengthy Honey Do list. But maintaining open lines of communication, checking in regularly, and collaborating closely with your partner throughout the execution process enables you to methodically work through DIY projects in a unified fashion. Shared accomplishments strengthen relationships.

Tips for Fostering Open Communication

- Schedule weekly or monthly progress review sessions to touch base.
- Be fully transparent about challenges encountered or concerns as they arise.
- Listen attentively to your partner's feedback and ideas.
- Compromise graciously if disagreements surface.
- Express appreciation for any help or flexibility offered.
- Share encouragement and praise progress; don't just critique.
- Keep discussions positive and solution focused.
- Infuse humor and celebrate victories to maintain morale.
- Manage frustration constructively if setbacks occur.
- Demonstrate respect for each other's limitations and comfort levels.
- Exchange gratitude for persevering together through the demanding parts.

By continuously communicating openly, honestly, and calmly with your spouse or partner when tackling DIY projects, you can achieve amazing home upgrades while simultaneously strengthening your relationship. The improvements become symbols of what you can accomplish together.

CASE STUDY: TODD AND JULIA'S DIY PRIORITIZATION JOURNEY

Todd and his wife, Julia, recently purchased a fixer-upper home needing many renovations. Julia eagerly created a Pinterest board to pin inspiration for upgrades in each room. Soon her digital ideas transformed into a handwritten Honey Do list on the fridge outlining dozens of desired projects.

Looking at the list, Todd felt overwhelmed and anxious. He didn't know where to start. "The projects ranged from quick paint jobs to major structural changes. I'm no contractor, so the list definitely intimidated me," he admitted.

The couple realized they needed to reset and reprioritize the tasks based on Todd's skill level, their schedules, and necessity. Safety and function took precedence over cosmetic improvements. They broke large endeavors like kitchen remodeling into smaller, distinct phases.

With an actionable plan based on open communication, Todd's anxiety eased. "Julia understanding my capabilities, and us tackling projects together rather than pushing all the work on me, made a world of difference," he said.

A year later, Todd has successfully checked off more than half the items off the once-intimidating list by methodically working through prioritized projects, enjoying a sense of accomplishment and teamwork with Julia along the way.

When facing a lengthy Honey Do list, deciding which tasks to tackle first can feel overwhelming. But proper project prioritization and planning sets you up for steady progress.

Priorities should be based on project urgency, complexity, seasonality, and dependencies. Critical home repairs take precedence over cosmetic upgrades. Larger endeavors should be broken into discrete phases.

The Family Handyman recommends grouping projects by room so you can fully complete upgrades efficiently. This avoids constantly shifting between tasks and locations (Family Handyman, 2023).

Effective prioritization also requires open communication with your partner. Discuss motivations behind requested projects and ideal timeframes. Compromise if you differ on urgency. Clarify responsibilities based on skills and workload capacity.

Creating a prioritized project schedule with milestones provides structure. Breaking large items into subtasks makes them feel less intimidating. Use apps to organize and collaborate, if desired.

Periodically review and realign priorities if new urgent issues emerge or situations change. Celebrate completed items to stay motivated. Proper planning prevents the list from feeling overwhelming.

With a pragmatic approach, patience, and teamwork, you can methodically work through projects together. Momentum and small wins will propel you forward.

Through upfront planning and open communication, we can thoughtfully pace ourselves in completing projects amidst the demands of daily life. Next, let's explore ways to maximize our limited time invested by working smart.

Maximizing Efficiency

When taking on home improvement projects, employing strategies to work as efficiently as possible will allow you to accomplish more in the limited spare time available. Wasting time hunting for tools, making extra trips to the hardware store, or dragging projects out over months leads to frustration. Thoughtful planning and preparation help maximize productivity.

Thoroughly review project instructions and watch online tutorial videos to understand each step before starting. Assemble all necessary tools, materials, and safety gear in one place to prevent interruptions (Family Handyman, 2023). Consider a checklist posted in the workspace.

For larger projects, break tasks into discrete stages that can be completed in short, focused work sessions. Define milestones upfront to maintain a sense of progress. Take photos after important steps to document building upon previous work.

Learn to use tools properly to avoid wasting time compensating for bad technique. For example, predrill holes when driving screws to prevent stripping screw heads. Keep tools sharp and clean for optimal performance (This Old House, 2010).

Set up an organized, uncluttered workspace. Good lighting, adequate electrical outlets, and a sturdy work surface allow efficiently moving through tasks. Store materials conveniently within reach. Designate specific spots for tools to enable finding them quickly.

Shop for materials wisely. Seek bulk discounts on frequently used fasteners and hardware. Buying excess leads to waste, while too little may require mid project store trips. Plan ahead to take advantage of seasonal sales (This Old House, 2009).

Working efficiently is a skill that improves over time as you refine systems and processes that suit your approach. But keeping productivity principles in mind from the start, even on initial projects, will help maximize your available time for home improvements.

MAXIMIZING EFFICIENCY ON DIY PROJECTS

Now that we've covered key project management strategies, maximizing efficiency is also crucial when taking on your Honey Do list. Finding ways to work smarter—not just harder

—can save significant amounts of time, effort, and money on home improvement endeavors.

When tackling DIY projects, every minute wasted equates to higher costs, both in terms of your limited personal time and actual financial expenditures. Identifying time-saving tricks and sticking to an efficient workflow keeps projects moving along briskly versus bogging down into prolonged battles.

Here are some tips for working as efficiently as possible.

Thoroughly Plan Out Each Step Before Starting

Taking time upfront to mentally envision and plan out each step of the project before starting the actual physical work can vastly improve efficiency down the line and prevent wasted efforts. Rushing into a project without thinking through the full process first often leads to costly mistakes, frustration, and unnecessary rework.

Declutter and Clean Your Workspace

Having a clear, clean, and organized work area prevents wasting precious time searching for tools or supplies, shifting clutter out of the way, or trying to work around a chaotic mess. Properly setting up your workspace helps maximize productivity.

Gather All Project Materials, Tools, and Hardware Beforehand

Ensuring you have all the necessary materials, tools, hardware, protective equipment, etc., conveniently on hand before starting work eliminates losing time later when you suddenly realize an item you need is missing. Scrambling to get missing pieces derails momentum.

Schedule Similar Projects Together When Possible

Try to batch and schedule projects requiring similar tasks together, when possible, to maximize your workflow. For example, it's most efficient to complete all kitchen cabinet painting together in one session rather than constantly shifting between different types of tasks.

Enlist Help From Others When Suitable

For larger, more complex DIY projects, enlist the help of a spouse, a family member or a friend, when suitable, to distribute the workload. What would take you two full weekends to complete may become a one-day job when you have an extra set of hands.

Avoid Sitting Idle Between Steps

Use any brief downtime between steps efficiently by getting set up and organized for the next task, sweeping up debris, sharpening tools, restocking supplies, and so on. Sitting too long, doing nothing, leads to losing momentum.

Learn Proper Tool Usage

Taking the time upfront to learn how to properly use tools not only keeps you safe but allows you to complete tasks faster and with fewer errors. Rushed or improper tool handling inevitably wastes precious time and energy.

Take Short Breaks at Logical Stopping Points

Remember to take short breaks for water, food, or to stretch at logical stopping points to refresh mentally and recover strength. Pushing to complete exhaustion decreases focus and increases the chance of sloppy mistakes.

By staying organized, planning thoroughly, moving briskly between steps, and working smarter rather than just grinding harder, you can get far more accomplished in less time. Proper preparation and locking in on efficiency make all the difference in successfully maximizing productivity throughout a project. Let's explore maximizing efficiency further through an insightful case study.

CASE STUDY: A TIME-CRUNCHED FATHER'S JOURNEY TO EFFICIENT PROJECT COMPLETION

Mike was a devoted father of two young kids, and he worked 50 hours a week. After getting home from his job, he prioritized spending quality time with his family in the evenings. However, Mike's wife, Jen, started pressuring him to finally tackle the ever-growing Honey Do list of home repairs he had been putting off for months.

The main project involved completely renovating an outdated downstairs bathroom. With his demanding work schedule, Mike knew that finishing the bathroom remodel efficiently in the few hours available on weekends would require focus and diligent preparation.

Here is how Mike maximized productivity to get the bathroom renovation completed in a timely manner:

- **Thorough planning:** Mike started by carefully reviewing online tutorials to understand the full scope and steps involved. He drew up detailed plans, mapping out each phase.
- **Advance organization:** The week before starting, Mike cleared out the entire bathroom and set up a folding table to hold all necessary tools and materials nearby.
- **Careful scheduling:** Mike planned the project in stages over four weekends to be completed between spending family time on the weekends.
- **Enlisting help:** Mike recruited his brother-in-law to assist with demo, so they could knock it out in a single Saturday.
- **Tool mastery:** Mike practiced using his borrowed tile saw ahead of time to be ready for quick, error-free cuts.

- **Focused work:** During each intense work session, Mike stayed on task between steps, cleaning up, restocking materials, and prepping the next phase.
- **Proper breaks:** Mike was careful to take five-minute water- and stretching breaks at milestones to recharge.

The result: Mike was able to completely transform the outdated bathroom into a gorgeous new space in less than a month by maximizing productivity from his limited weekend hours. Everything went smoothly and on schedule, thanks to diligent preparation and an efficiency mindset throughout.

THE EFFICIENCY MINDSET

Adopting an efficiency mindset is just as important as specific time-saving techniques when taking on DIY projects. How you mentally approach tasks greatly impacts your speed, quality, and enjoyment of the process.

Following are ways to cultivate an efficiency mindset:

Always look for areas of waste in a process. Then seek ways to eliminate unnecessary steps.

- Are you making redundant measurements or miscuts leading to rework?
- Is lack of planning resulting in forgotten items mid project?
- Can tools/materials be organized to reduce search time?

Aim to strike the optimal balance between speed and precision.

- Rushing leads to frustration through mistakes, while obsessive precision causes delays.
- Strive for accuracy within smart time budgets to increase velocity.

Break free of perfectionism tendencies hindering progress.

- Repetitive small tune-ups to get something "just right" often produce diminishing returns.
- Remember that done is better than perfect. Projects can always be revisited.
- Focus on major milestones first, then refine as needed.

Identify your peak productivity hours and protect them.

- Block off your most focused morning hours for intense project work.
- Use late afternoons for organizing or clean-up tasks requiring less mental sharpness.

Find ways to integrate efficiency into leisure, as well.

- Apply the mindset when completing household chores and errands.
- Evaluate your routines for wasted motion and unnecessary activities.

- Free up more weekend time for passion projects.

Leverage technology to remove redundant work.

- Use smartphone apps to digitize recurring tasks like shopping lists or punch lists.
- Invest in smart power tools with automated features, precision sensing, and connectivity.
- Enable voice commands to play music, set timers, and adjust lighting hands-free.

Surround yourself with other efficiency-minded people.

- Their enthusiasm is contagious, and you'll share tips.
- Inefficiency drags everyone down, so choose colleagues wisely.

Making efficiency a habit will transform how you approach DIY and life overall. You'll achieve greater work-life balance while also becoming more proficient at the tasks you care about most.

When taking on home improvement projects, working efficiently is crucial to saving time, money, and effort while achieving quality results. Finding ways to minimize waste and streamline your process leads to faster project completion.

Proper planning and preparation prevent problems down the line, according to experts. Take time up front to analyze required steps, materials, and tools to avoid mid project delays (Family Handyman, 2023).

Decluttering your workspace also maximizes efficiency by clearing obstacles that slow you down. Stage all necessary materials and tools within reach to prevent wasting time searching later.

Look for ways to work in batches on repetitive tasks like painting trim or drilling cabinet hardware. Tackle similar jobs together to maximize focus and workflow.

Enlist help from others on suitable projects to distribute the workload. Two people can lift heavy materials and hold items in place more easily than one.

Avoid sitting idle between steps. Use this time to start cleanup, organize materials for the next task, or take a short rest to boost energy.

Learning to use tools properly improves speed and quality. Rushed or improper technique wastes effort. Follow manufacturer instructions.

By staying organized, planning thoroughly, and working smarter rather than harder, you can achieve greater efficiency on DIY projects, saving money and getting better outcomes.

TIME-SAVING TIPS AND TRICKS FOR DIY PROJECTS

When it comes to home improvement projects, time is money. The longer tasks take to complete, the more they can end up costing you in terms of both materials and labor. Finding ways to work efficiently is the key to successfully completing your Honey Do list without wasting precious personal time and financial resources.

As the old carpentry saying goes, "Measure twice, cut once." Taking a little extra time upfront to properly plan and prepare for a project can ultimately save you hours of effort down the line. Rushing headfirst into a DIY task without thoroughly thinking through each step is a recipe for frustration and mistakes.

Here are some tips for maximizing productivity and efficiency on DIY home projects.

Have a Game Plan

- Take time to map out the full scope of the project and every step involved before starting.
- Create a written plan detailing the process from start to finish.
- Gather all necessary materials, tools, and supplies in advance so everything is on hand.
- Mentally visualize yourself completing each phase. Proper prep gets your mind ready.

Clear the Decks

- Declutter and clean your workspace to prevent wasting time later shifting piles of stuff around.
- Remove obstacles, clutter, and furniture from the surrounding work area and pathways.
- Work cleanly and efficiently without constant impediments in your way.

Get Organized and Tool Up

- Organize your tools so everything has a designated storage spot and is easily accessible when needed.
- Avoid wasting time searching for a specific drill bit or blade during a project.
- Check tool condition and restock consumables like sandpaper, screws, and batteries.

Work in Batches

- Tackle all DIY projects of the same type at once, when possible, rather than bouncing randomly between tasks.
- For example, complete all bathroom tiling in a single session, instead of tiling, painting, then returning to tiling.

Enlist Help for Two-Person Tasks

Having an extra set of hands can vastly reduce the time required for jobs that require two people to maneuver heavy objects or reach tricky spaces.

Keep Your Momentum

- After finishing a task, switch gears to the next required step rather than sitting idle. Avoid productivity killing downtime or distractions.
- Power through your timeline but take mini breaks at logical task boundaries to recharge.

Clean as You Go

- Frequently deal with dust, debris, scraps, trash, and other items to prevent dangerous slippery piles and suffocating air.
- A tidy workspace maintains morale and focus. Cleaning up later takes exponentially longer.

Take Proper Breaks

- Schedule short water, snack, and stretching breaks after completing milestone steps.
- Brief breathers help boost mental clarity and physical energy levels for powering through the next stage. Don't overexert.

Ask for Guidance From Experts

- Learn handy tricks and time-tested techniques from experienced contractors or friends to avoid rookie mistakes.
- Invest time up front consulting tutorials and how-to guides to master proper methodology.

Invest in Quality Tools and Materials

Properly investing in quality tools and construction materials can vastly improve efficiency over trying to force subpar equipment to work.

By staying organized, planning thoroughly, moving briskly between steps, and working smarter rather than just grinding harder, you can get far more accomplished in less time. Proper preparation and locking in on efficiency make all the difference in successfully maximizing productivity throughout a project.

Let's explore this concept through two examples.

CASE STUDY 1: JOHN'S TIME-SAVING STRATEGIES

John was eager to finally tackle various leftover house projects that had been lingering for months on his Honey Do list. But with limited spare time on evenings and weekends due to family obligations, he knew he couldn't afford to waste a single minute to disorganization, distraction, or delays.

John leveraged various time-saving strategies to maximize productivity by:

- making a detailed list of every project and step needed in priority order.
- setting up a temporary workshop in the garage to store all necessary tools and materials.
- enlisting his wife's help to speed up painting and demolition.
- completing all tiling tasks sequentially before shifting to drywall repairs.
- staging materials for each phase nearby to avoid hunting around.
- setting a kitchen timer to take short breaks every two hours.
- asking a contractor friend for tips to avoid rookie tiling mistakes.
- focusing intensely on each task to avoid being sidetracked.
- picking up debris frequently so it wouldn't snowball into a huge mess.

By staying focused and working efficiently without wasting time, John was amazed at how much he was able to accomplish in just a few weekends of concentrated effort.

CASE STUDY 2: TODD'S BASEMENT RENOVATION TIME-SAVERS

Todd had a massive basement-renovation project on his hands, including framing new walls, running electric, installing drywall, painting, and installing new flooring throughout the 1,000-square-foot space. He knew going in that careful planning would be crucial to finishing in a reasonable timeframe.

After thoroughly planning out each step, Todd started by drawing up a detailed project schedule with milestones. He researched the optimal methods and order of operations online.

Knowing dust control would be a challenge, Todd rented a powerful shop vac to frequently contain drywall dust before it spread. He also purchased high-quality power tools, like a drywall screw gun, to speed up labor intensive tasks.

Todd resisted the urge to multitask too much. "I focused on completing each step fully before moving on to the next phase. This prevented having half-finished tasks dragging on," he said.

By applying savvy time-saving techniques, Todd completed the major renovation in just a few weekends. His wife was thrilled with the results and impressed by his efficiency.

KEY TAKEAWAYS ON MAXIMIZING PRODUCTIVITY

- Proper up-front planning prevents delays and errors down the line.
- Decluttering your path clears the way for brisk workflow.
- Staging tools and materials nearby eliminates wasted motion.
- Working in phases streamlines focus on each task.
- Using the proper tools for each job improves speed and quality.
- Resisting multitasking prevents lingering loose ends.
- Short breaks maintain mental focus and prevent exhaustion.
- Research and expert input help avoid rookie mistakes.
- Efficiency leads to faster and often better end results.

ADDITIONAL TIME-SAVING STRATEGIES

Here are some additional tips for increasing efficiency and productivity on DIY projects:

- **Build modular components when feasible.** Construct sheds, benches, organizers, and more in easily movable sections for simplicity and flexibility.
- **Utilize precut materials.** Dimensional lumber, plywood, PVC boards, and more are available precut to standard sizes to skip cutting.

- **Choose low-maintenance building materials.** Composite decking, fiber cement siding, LED lighting, and more require less upkeep over time.
- **Automate repetitive tasks.** Programmable thermostats, smart locks, automatic pet feeders, and more remove daily chores.
- **Streamline landscaping maintenance.** Install drip irrigation, native plants, zoysia grass, mulch paths, and other low-upkeep features.
- **Purchase multifunction power tools.** Look for saws, drivers, and more that convert for multiple uses.
- **Rent or borrow infrequently used specialty tools.** Owning every tool is unnecessary for the occasional user.
- **Preassembly saves installation time.** Opt for furniture, storage items, swing sets, and more that come already assembled.
- **Hire out skilled labor when appropriate.** Some complex projects, like electrical, which can be dangerous, are best left to experts.

When taking on home improvement projects, every minute saved is money earned. Completing tasks faster allows you to take on more projects over time. Here are some tips and tricks to maximize productivity:

- Create detailed plans and gather all materials needed upfront. This preparation prevents delays once work begins.

- Only focus on one project area at a time. Constantly shifting between rooms decreases focus.
- Stage tools, supplies, and hardware within reach of the workspace to avoid wasting time searching midproject.
- Set up an efficient workflow and containment plan for dust and debris to minimize cleanup time.
- Use quality power tools with features like adjustable speed triggers for improved control and faster progress.
- Learn the proper techniques for using both hand- and power tools. Mistakes waste time and effort.
- Work in batches by completing all jobs of one type before moving to another.
- Enlist help for suitable projects. Two people can lift, hold, and construct faster than one.
- Take short breaks to refresh mental clarity and physical stamina at logical stopping points.
- Invest in convenience upgrades like self-closing taps, soft-close hinges, and automated lighting.

By applying specialized tools, proper planning, and efficient workflow, you can reduce project duration, fatigue, and errors. Working smarter maximizes productivity.

Beyond just individual gains in productivity, completing DIY tasks jointly also presents fertile opportunities to strengthen our most vital partnership.

Make a Difference with Your Review
Unlock the Power of DIY Mastery

"Success is not final, failure is not fatal: It is the courage to continue that counts."

— WINSTON S. CHURCHILL

People who embark on the journey of DIY projects not only transform their homes but also cultivate a sense of accomplishment and purpose. To make this empowering experience accessible to everyone, we're on a mission. And you, dear reader, play a crucial role in achieving it.

Would you extend a helping hand to someone in need, even if it meant no recognition for yourself?

Meet the struggling DIY enthusiast – someone just like you once were. Eager to make a difference but unsure where to start. Our mission is to make DIY mastery accessible to everyone, and we need your support.

Most people judge a book by its cover and reviews. So here's our ask on behalf of a fellow DIY enthusiast you've never met:

Please help that aspiring DIYer by leaving a review for "The Honey Do List For Guys DIY Made Easy."

Your gift costs nothing and takes less than 60 seconds but can change a fellow DIYer's life forever. Your review could help...

...one more homeowner transformed their space.

...one more beginner becomes a DIY expert.

...one more family bond over a successful project.

...one more individual finds purpose in DIY.

To experience the 'feel-good' sensation and genuinely help this person, all you have to do is leave a review.

Simply scan the QR code to share your thoughts:

If you feel good about assisting a faceless DIY enthusiast, welcome to the club. You're one of us.

I'm that much more excited to help you tackle DIY projects more efficiently than you can possibly imagine. You'll love the tips and strategies I'm about to share in the coming chapters.

Thank you from the bottom of my heart. Now, back to our DIY adventure.

• Your biggest fan, Brent Sniper

PS - Fun fact: By sharing valuable insights, you become more valuable to others. If you believe this book will help a fellow DIY enthusiast, pass it their way.

Partner Participation and Collaboration

While DIY projects may seem like solitary pursuits, finding ways to involve your spouse or partner can be hugely rewarding for your relationship as well as the quality of the finished product. Collaboration brings a wider range of skills and ideas to the table. And working together toward a shared goal deepens intimacy and connection.

Openly communicate about your interests, abilities, and limitations related to DIY and home repairs. Look for opportunities to take on projects that play to each of your strengths and provide chances to learn from each other (HomeTun, 2023).

Involve your partner in the full process, from initial brainstorming sessions to gathering materials to the hands-on work. Maintain enthusiastic participation, even during frustrating stages of projects. Share small wins along the way (This Old House, 2009).

Find ways you can actively assist, even if your partner takes the lead. Help with demolition, cleaning up debris, fetching tools or supplies, and providing snacks to maintain energy levels. Offer praise and encouragement.

Compromise when disagreements arise over design elements. Blend your styles into a cohesive finished product you're both proud of. Recognize when to seek outside opinions to settle disputes.

Share responsibilities based on skillsets, not gender roles. Women can be great at carpentry or wiring. Men may excel at upholstery or decorative touches. Let go of assumptions (Liu, 2023).

Working collaboratively allows you to take on more ambitious efforts neither could tackle alone. The journey bonds you through shared effort and you'll gain confidence as a DIY team poised to upgrade your home.

BENEFITS OF TEAMWORK ON DIY PROJECTS

"Teamwork makes the dream work." This popular saying rings very true when applying it to tackling home improvement projects together with your partner. Traditionally, the Honey Do list may have you cast in the sole role of household handyman. However, choosing to involve your other half in the process can provide tremendous benefits for both your relationship and the quality of the finished products.

Collaborating on DIY tasks as a team can enrich your partnership in multiple ways:

- Fostering open communication and compromise
- Playing to each of your unique strengths and interests
- Learning new skills together
- Bonding through shared accomplishments
- Taking pride in improving your home as a united front
- Lightening the workload through cooperation

The key to harmonious teamwork is approaching project participation with an open mindset focused on interest and ability rather than outdated gender-based assumptions. Create opportunities for both partners to do the following:

- Learn basic handyman skills together like proper tool usage, safety precautions, and so on
- Research, plan, and thoughtfully talk through project steps as a team
- Share in physical tasks based on comfort level and capability
- Leverage each other's natural strengths and preferences
- Discuss any issues openly, and compromise as needed
- Provide encouragement and celebrate joint victories

With cooperation, clear communication, patience, and a willingness to learn from each other, DIY projects can strengthen your partnership immensely while also enhancing your living space. Let's explore some of the top benefits of embracing team-work in detail.

Improved Communication and Compromise

Completing DIY projects requires reviewing plans together, checking in frequently during work, and openly discussing any issues that arise. This fosters direct communication, expressing needs, and reaching compromises, which are invaluable relationship skills.

Playing to Individual Strengths

We all have diverse talents. Maybe one excels at building things but dislikes finishing work. The other pays great attention to detail when painting but struggles with carpentry. Embrace these differences by dividing and conquering tasks accordingly.

Learning Together

Approach projects as an opportunity for each partner to gain hands-on experience with guidance from the other. Demonstrate proper use of tools and techniques to support the learning process. Growth takes patience but builds confidence.

Shared Sense of Accomplishment

Celebrate successes, like a newly tiled bathroom or repainted exterior, as a team. Collaboration leads to shared pride and appreciation in outcomes that can only be achieved together through hard work.

Lightening the Load

Two sets of hands make quick work of physically demanding tasks like demolition, lugging materials, and cleanup. What may take one person days can be accomplished in an afternoon together.

Bonding Experience

Time spent creating something meaningful together—filled with laughter, learning, sweat, and likely a few mistakes along the way—forges deep bonds. The whole process becomes about more than just the end result.

Things to Keep in Mind

- Don't force it if there isn't genuine interest. Some may prefer to just cheer from the sidelines.
- Be patient with the learning curve. Confidence builds gradually through guided practice.
- Trade off tedious tasks to share the workload. Split up larger projects into batches.
- Discuss needs openly. Compromise on design elements that leave both parties satisfied.
- Leverage different perspectives. More ideas lead to better solutions.

- Have fun! Infuse humor and positivity into the experience.

While tackling the Honey Do list solo may seem habitual, making a conscious effort to involve your partner more collaboratively can lead to big payoffs for your relationship, upgraded living space, and mutual growth. The sense of teamwork and shared purpose make chores into cherished memories.

STRATEGIES FOR WORKING TOGETHER EFFECTIVELY ON DIY PROJECTS

While teamwork provides tremendous benefits, successfully collaborating on DIY projects requires intention, open communication, and a willingness to compromise. Discuss the project scope up front and continue checking in throughout the process to ensure you work efficiently as a team. Some helpful strategies are listed next.

Agree on the Project Scope and Timeline

- Gather inspiration photos and examples that appeal to both your styles.
- List must-have features versus nice-to-haves.
- Agree on a design direction and specific elements to include.
- Make a comprehensive list of required steps and materials.

- Discuss how to split up tasks based on interests and strengths.
- Set a realistic timeline, accounting for other obligations.
- Commit to regular check-ins on progress and any issues.

Research Options and Make a Budget

- Read DIY guides to understand the full scope of work and prep needed.
- Watch online tutorial videos to ensure the project is within your skill level.
- Comparison-shop materials and tools to balance cost with quality.
- Get multiple quotes from specialty contractors, if needed.
- Create a comprehensive budget with a 10–20% contingency fund.
- Review the budget together and get aligned before purchasing anything.

Take Safety Precautions

- Carefully check for and disconnect electrical, water, and gas lines.
- Purchase all recommended PPE like goggles, respirators, and ear protection.

- Ensure ladders are secure, scaffolding is braced, and power tools are grounded,
- Check tool and equipment condition; repair or replace damaged items.
- Keep a first aid kit and a fire extinguisher within reach.
- Set up cord protectors, safety cones, barricades, and drop cloths.

Secure Permits and Arrange Inspections

- Research permit requirements based on the type and scope of the project.
- Submit proper permit applications, including all required plans and documentation. Every city and county has different requirements.
- Schedule any required inspections at milestone stages.
- Verify finished work meets all applicable building codes.

Determine When to Hire Specialty Help

- Outsource work requiring expertise like electrical, plumbing, or engineering.
- Consider hiring for intensive manual labor like demolition or hauling debris.
- Bring in extra hands for fussy finish work like drywall mudding or tiling.
- Discuss when it makes financial sense to hire specialty help vs DIY.

Compromise and Communicate Openly

- Check in frequently and discuss any issues or changes in plans.
- Accommodate each other's preferences when possible.
- Divide tedious tasks equitably and trade off as needed.
- Ask questions rather than make assumptions.
- Be patient and willing to explain concepts or teach skills.
- Show appreciation for each other's contributions.

By getting aligned up front, openly communicating, and tapping in to each other's strengths throughout the process, you'll be equipped to work together as an effective DIY team. United in purpose, a challenging project becomes a shared adventure that brings you closer together.

CAPITALIZING ON COMPLEMENTARY STRENGTHS IN DIY PROJECTS

Chances are each partner naturally offers different strengths and capabilities that can contribute to an efficient and successful project outcome. Take time to have an open discussion about your individual attributes. Consider the following:

- **Physical capabilities:** One partner may excel at strenuous tasks requiring strength, stamina, and endurance such as demolition, hauling materials, digging, and so on.

- **Technical proficiency:** You may find one partner feels more adept at using power tools, performing repairs, or handling complex installations.
- **Artistic eye:** When it comes to aesthetics like painting, tiling, landscaping, and decorating, one of you likely has superior talents.
- **Research skills:** Carefully reviewing how-to guides, watching tutorials, and sourcing ideas may come more naturally to one partner.
- **Project management:** Developing timelines, tracking budgets, and coordinating schedules are organizational skills one person may handle best.
- **Budgeting:** One partner could have superior abilities for smartly managing finances, finding deals, and estimating costs.

Rather than feeling solely responsible for all aspects of a project, openly recognize each other's individual strengths. Then strategically delegate tasks accordingly to maximize efficiency.

This team mentality allows you to achieve results faster and often better than flying solo. Then be sure to celebrate your shared accomplishments together.

Tips for Capitalizing on Complementary Strengths

- Have an open discussion about each person's abilities and interests.
- List all the tasks required to complete the desired project.
- Align tasks to each partner's strengths without overgeneralizing gender roles.
- Split up less desirable tasks so one person isn't stuck with all the drudgery.
- Check ego and sincerely acknowledge areas where your partner excels beyond your own ability.
- Learn from each other—use this as an opportunity to expand your skills as well through collaboration.
- Provide encouragement and appreciation for each other's contributions.
- Communicate any guidance needed clearly without micromanaging.
- Review progress regularly, provide feedback, and adapt plans as needed.
- Upon completion, emphasize successes as shared team accomplishments.

While becoming well-rounded is valuable, also embrace the power of partnerships. Combining diverse, complementary capabilities and insights allows you to achieve incredible outcomes together.

Appreciate Different Perspectives

Partners often bring different perspectives to the table based on their background and personality, which can enhance the creative process when designing and executing projects.

By incorporating diverse vantage points, the end result is often greater than the sum of its parts. Keep communicating, and course-correct along the way.

LEARNING TOGETHER AND BONDING THROUGH DIY PROJECTS

Another major benefit of tackling DIY projects jointly is the opportunity it provides for both partners to learn new skills together. Rather than automatically deferring specialized tasks to whoever seems more experienced, use joint projects as a chance to expand each other's capabilities.

Select projects strategically that allow you both to:

- gain hands-on experience operating new power tools or using new techniques.
- develop competence with intimidating tasks like tiling, carpentry, drywall, and electrical.
- build familiarity with common DIY terminology, methodologies, and best practices.
- study how-to guides, illustrations, and watch online video tutorials together prior to starting.

You can further bond in the learning process by:

- visiting home improvement stores together to select project materials.
- collaboratively developing the project plans, timeline, budgets, and so on.
- assisting with basic but essential prep and clean-up tasks before/after work sessions.
- providing refreshments, snacks and encouragement during intense project periods.
- sharing constructive feedback and praise on each other's progress.

The key is looking at the overall project as an egalitarian team effort regardless of individual roles. Both parties should participate in whatever way they feel capable and comfortable at their existing skill level. But remain open-minded to inspiration that may emerge from your partner. Over time as knowledge builds, you may be motivated to take on more complex hands-on elements that once seemed intimidating or unapproachable.

Tips for Optimizing Joint Learning

- Openly communicate each person's experience level to set appropriate expectations.
- Take time to explain concepts thoroughly and answer all questions.
- Be patient with the learning curve; competency develops gradually.

- Break larger tasks into smaller achievable steps when teaching skills.
- Praise each other's focus, effort, and improvements to build confidence.
- Trade off trying new tools and techniques to gain firsthand experience.
- Start conservatively but challenge each other to expand comfort zones.
- Review results together and exchange constructive suggestions.
- Share learning resources and guides that were helpful.

By embracing an open, encouraging mindset, DIY projects become an opportunity to learn alongside your partner at every experience level. You return the favor for the guidance they once provided you. Growth deepens mutual respect and attraction.

Strengthening Bonds Along the Way

More than just the hands-on work itself, bonds are strengthened by the overall collaborative process of seeing a project through together:

Joint Planning

- Brainstorming design ideas that incorporate both your visions
- Drawing rough project sketches together
- Estimating expenses and creating a shared budget

Material Selection

- Browsing Pinterest and Houzz for inspiring photos
- Visiting home improvement stores to select finishes and components
- Compromising on decor elements based on both your tastes

Ongoing Teamwork and Assistance

- One partner tackling labor-intensive tasks while the other provides refreshments and encouragement
- Switching roles periodically to offer breaks and vary the workload
- Providing reminders as extra eyes checking for safety or quality

Celebrating Success

- Admiring the improvements and functionality added by your shared efforts
- Reminiscing over laughs and memorable moments throughout the process
- Discussing lessons learned to build on for future projects

By fully sharing in the experience—from planning through problem-solving to celebration—you amplify feelings of accomplishment and camaraderie.

Mixing Sweat Equity With Cooperation in DIY Projects

While teamwork lightens the load, certain home improvement tasks inevitably require greater physical exertion and "sweat equity." Partners can thoughtfully play to their individual strengths and comfort levels when dividing up the more hands-on physical workload.

For larger or more strenuous projects, consider the following:

- Having one partner tackle the more strength-focused tasks like demolition, digging, lifting heavy materials, and so on.
- The other partner handles precision-focused elements like finishing trim, cabinetry, tiling, painting, and so on.
- Switching roles occasionally so you both gain experience with the different types of labor involved. Variety is enriching.

When managing physically demanding aspects, be sure to consider these steps:

- Use proper safety gear and proper technique to prevent muscular or repetitive stress injuries. Lift with legs, brace core, avoid twisting, and so on.
- Take regular breaks to avoid overexertion and fatigue. Drink water and rest muscles.
- Stay hydrated and nourish with protein-rich snacks to maintain energy levels. Quick fuels like dried fruits or

protein bars help counter depletion.

- Check in often and watch for signs of burnout. Stop when exhaustion sets in. Pace the work over multiple days, if needed.

No single project or duty exclusively defines you or your contribution. Support each other, be flexible, and communicate openly about physical limits or frustrations. With empathy and cooperation, you ease the labor burden and foster greater mutual understanding and respect.

A Source of Shared Pride and Accomplishment

Approaching DIY as an egalitarian joint endeavor cultivates a sense of shared identity and pride centered around your home. The house becomes an embodiment of your combined efforts. You created something special as a team that neither could have achieved alone as seamlessly.

This feeling of shared accomplishment and ownership stems from:

- successfully achieving a complex task requiring both of your unique contributions.

- significantly elevating the aesthetics and function of your living space through upgrades only made possible together.
- instilling confidence in both parties by learning and developing new hands-on skills as a couple.
- saving substantial money over hiring professional contractors to complete projects.

You'll enjoy the tangible fruits of your shared labor every day as it directly enhances the comfort of your daily lives and memories made in the home. This builds immense satisfaction along with the intimacy forged through collaborating constructively to enrich your space. Continue strengthening that bond as you proudly enjoy the results of your teamwork for years to come.

CASE STUDY: MARY AND JONATHAN'S TEAMWORK TRANSFORMATION

When Mary presented her eager husband Jonathan with a Honey Do list, his face dropped. "I felt completely overwhelmed. How could I take on all these major home upgrades alone?" he asked.

Previously, Jonathan tried completing projects solo, struggling through the labor and learning as he went. Mary, thinking home improvement "just wasn't her thing," stayed uninvolved.

But for this latest list, Mary offered to work as Jonathan's partner from planning to execution. "I didn't need to hammer and saw to provide valuable help," she explained.

Mary researched materials and prices together with Jonathan. She assisted with demolition prep and cleanup. During breaks she brought water and healthy snacks to keep Jonathan's energy up.

Rather than hand off directives, Mary framed the experience as an opportunity for couple bonding and growth. The positive collaborative environment allowed them to tackle far bigger projects than Jonathan could solo.

"Working together made these improvements feel like shared accomplishments we can both take pride in," said Jonathan. "Our home and relationship are stronger than ever, thanks to teamwork."

With the proper approach, motivation, and teamwork, DIY projects can strengthen your relationship while also enhancing your living space. Here are some tips:

- Involve your partner in planning, research, budgeting, and project selection.
- Divide tasks based on interest and abilities, not gender.
- Take time to teach each other new skills.
- Compromise on timeline and priorities.
- Provide lots of encouragement and celebrate joint victories.
- Reframe projects positively as opportunities for quality time together.

By embracing an open, communicative mindset, you can work cooperatively as a couple to complete projects you'd struggle with alone. Share in the labor and in the satisfaction of a job well done.

Beyond beautification, a wealth of savings and satisfactions stem from acquiring select repair skills ourselves rather than reflexively hiring help.

Mastering Home Repairs

When faced with a broken appliance, leaky pipe, or other home repair needs, your first instinct may be to call a professional. But equipping yourself with the skills and knowledge to tackle common fixes and upgrades can save significant time and money. With proper preparation and guidance, you can master many basic home repairs.

First, assess your comfort level and capabilities honestly. Building confidence takes time. Start small with easy repairs before attempting more complex electrical or plumbing jobs (Family Handyman, 2023).

Next, assemble a well-stocked toolbox with essential supplies. A solid toolkit tailored to common tasks like hanging items, assembling furniture, patching walls, and minor installations enables efficiently completing repairs. Invest in quality to avoid frustration (This Old House, 2010).

Study manufacturer instructions, warranty information, and user manuals thoroughly before beginning repairs. For household appliances, understanding proper operations can prevent unnecessary mistakes. Consulting manuals also provides insightful maintenance tips (Consumer Affairs, 2023).

For many repairs, step-by-step online tutorials are invaluable resources. Watch videos to grasp techniques before starting. Pausing as you go enables mimicking shown procedures. Seek multiple explanations of complex fixes to reinforce techniques.

Don't allow initial minor missteps to become major setbacks. Mistakes happen during the learning process. Focus on figuring out solutions rather than dwelling on errors. Successful DIY involves creative problem solving.

Be willing to call in professional assistance if you reach the limits of your skills and comfort zone. But don't quit at the first hiccup. Pushing past frustrations leads to growth. Over time, you may be surprised what repairs become second nature.

DIY HOME REPAIRS

Home repairs and maintenance work can be extremely expensive if you hire professional handymen, electricians, plumbers, and contractors. According to HomeAdvisor, the average hourly rate for a general handyman is $65–$90 per hour (HomeAdvisor, 2022). And for specialty work like plumbing or electrical repairs, costs often exceed $100 per hour with minimum service charges.

These high labor rates motivate many homeowners to learn how to tackle repairs themselves through DIY. The good news is that with proper guidance, investing in some key tools, and getting hands-on practice, you can successfully complete many basic repair tasks around your home.

While intensive electrical and plumbing jobs are best left to licensed professionals, an array of routine maintenance and minor fixes can be managed DIY everything from patching drywall to replacing sink fixtures to installing new flooring. Certain repairs may require getting a building permit, and you want to ensure any work meets code requirements. But aside from complicated rewiring, installing new circuits, or opening up walls, many common repairs are within reach.

Follow these tips to master common fixes:

- **Diagnose the problem.** Determine the exact issue and what is causing it. Observation is key.
- **Do your research.** Consult repair guides, videos, and experts to understand the full process and technique.
- **Gather supplies.** Make sure you have all necessary tools, materials, and replacement parts beforehand.
- **Remember safety first.** Use proper protective gear like gloves, goggles, and masks and take other precautionary measures.
- **Follow instructions.** Refer back to repair guides and photos as you work. Don't rely on memory.
- **Document the process.** Take photos and notes at each step for future reference.

- **Ask for help, if needed.** Don't be afraid to recruit an experienced friend for coaching.
- **Be patient.** Some repairs take time and practice to master. Avoid frustration.
- **Start small.** Build confidence with easy fixes before tackling bigger, more complex jobs.
- **Take pride in your work.** Successfully completing repairs fosters a great sense of accomplishment.

With the right approach, common home repairs like patching drywall, fixing leaky faucets, replacing light fixtures, and more are doable for any motivated DIYer willing to learn. Let's explore some of the most common DIY repairs.

Drywall Repairs

Holes in drywall can result from hanging pictures, shelves, or TV mounts. Luckily, small holes are relatively simple for a novice to patch. Following is how to do just that:

- Wear gloves, goggles, and a dust mask for protection.
- Use a utility knife to cut away loose material around the hole into a square or rectangle.
- Cut a drywall patch slightly larger than the hole. Secure with drywall screws.
- Apply joint compound over the seams using a putty knife. Let dry and sand smooth.
- Prime and paint the patch to match the existing wall color.

Larger holes or water damage may require cutting entire drywall sheets for replacement. Take proper fire-safety precautions if wiring is exposed.

Fixing Leaky Faucets

The annoying drip of a leaky faucet can waste hundreds of gallons of water over time. Fixing this yourself saves money over a plumber. Here's how to do it:

- Turn off water supply lines and open the faucet to relieve pressure.
- Disassemble the faucet handle and valve to access washers and O-rings.
- Replace worn rubber parts that cause drips. Use valve grease on reassembly.
- Turn water back on slowly to check for leaks. Tighten connections, if needed.
- Replace handles, turn water on fully, and test operation.

Leaky Pipe Repairs

Pipes can spring slow leaks over time due to corrosion, freezing, joints loosening, and more. But replacing a section is doable:

- Turn off main water supply. Drain plumbing lines.
- Cut out the damaged section of pipe.

- Measure and cut replacement pipe to fit with couplings.
- Connect new pipe with coupling fittings. Seal threads with Teflon tape.
- Turn water back on slowly and check for leaks.

Shutting off the main supply before repairs is crucial to prevent water damage.

Replacing a Light Fixture

Upgrading outdated light fixtures provides a quick visual impact. Use caution and turn off power at the breaker when replacing:

- Take photos of wiring connections before disconnecting.
- Disconnect wires and remove old fixture mount plate from electrical box.
- Install new fixture mount plate and make wiring connections.
- Attach new fixture to mount plate. Maintain wire connections inside junction box.
- Restore power and test fixture operation. Update wall switch, if needed.

Safety should be the top priority. A professional electrician can assist if you are uncomfortable working with wiring.

Replacing a Toilet

With proper planning and preparation, replacing an outdated or malfunctioning toilet is a manageable DIY project:

- Turn off toilet water supply and flush to empty tank. Sponge remaining water.
- Disconnect and remove supply line. Unbolt toilet from floor flange. Remove toilet.
- Scrape old wax from toilet flange. Install new wax ring.
- Lower new toilet onto flange, aligning bolts with holes. Hand tighten nuts onto bolts.
- Reconnect water supply and turn on. Test for leaks and stability before fully tightening bolts.

Modern efficient toilets install much the same but require less water per flush. Always use a new wax ring for optimal sealing.

THE COST SAVINGS OF DIY

It's astonishing how much money you can save by doing home repairs and installations yourself rather than hiring a professional. For example:

- **Replacing 10 windows:** Contractor cost $5,000, DIY cost $2,000 (60% savings)
- **Installing laminate flooring in 2 rooms:** Contractor cost $3,600, DIY cost $1,200 (67% savings)

- **Building a new wooden deck:** Contractor cost $7,000, DIY cost $1,800 (74% savings)
- **Painting the interior of a 2,000-square-foot home:** Contractor cost $4,000, DIY cost $500 (88% savings)
- **Installing new bathroom vanity and fixtures:** Contractor cost $2,800, DIY cost $450 (84% savings)
- **Adding interior doors and trim:** Contractor cost $3,600, DIY cost $900 (75% savings)
- **Building a privacy fence:** Contractor cost $5,400, DIY cost $1,600 (70% savings)

Even basic handyman services like painting, building shelves, or hanging TVs cost at least $65 per hour hired out. But with a trip to the hardware store and a free YouTube tutorial, you can gain new skills and keep the cash in your wallet.

Safety Considerations

While the cost incentives of DIY are compelling, safety should remain the top priority:

- Use caution when working with electricity—turn off power at main breaker panel.
- Wear protective gear like safety goggles, dust masks, ear protection, gloves, and boots.
- Ensure ladders or scaffolding are on stable, level surfaces and brace properly.
- Follow manufacturer instructions closely for power tools and chemicals.

- Work in well-ventilated areas and use drop cloths when painting.
- Lifting heavy materials risks back injuries—use proper form or get help.
- Prevent power tool and falling risks by avoiding fatigue and staying focused.
- Keep fire extinguishers and first aid kits in reach.
- Disconnect appliances before plumbing repairs to avoid electric shocks.

While seemingly daunting at first, basic home repairs simply require methodically following step-by-step instructions paired with safety diligence. Acquiring specialized tools expands the realm of DIY possibilities over time.

Building Confidence in Repairs

Gaining confidence in home repair skills requires patience and hands-on practice. Consider these tips to systematically build competence:

- Start by assisting family and friends with repairs to learn techniques.
- Tackle easy repairs like hardware, leaky pipes, loose tiles, or patching holes.
- Follow online video tutorials carefully for each type of repair.
- Invest in tools needed for common issues around your home.

- Attempt repairs first in inconspicuous areas to allow mistakes.
- Document "lessons learned" after finishing jobs to improve next time.
- Build knowledge of building codes to ensure proper installation.
- Know when to call a professional—some jobs, like electrical, are specialized.
- Seek opportunities to expand knowledge through courses at local hardware stores.

Passing down repair skills also accelerates learning. Learn side-by-side with kids to teach them fundamentals. Repetition develops muscle memory and the confidence required to efficiently tackle repairs.

Over time, advancing from trivially simple repairs to more complex improvements builds competence. Maintaining a well-stocked toolbox equipped for common issues also prepares you to act quickly whenever something breaks or requires maintenance.

PRIORITIZING HOME MAINTENANCE

Performing routine maintenance on your home is one of the most important things you can do as a homeowner. Regular preventative care helps avoid far more costly emergency repairs down the road. Make diligent home maintenance a top priority by proactively inspecting, servicing, repairing, and upgrading components before problems arise.

Replacing Consumables on Schedule

Many home components are designed as consumables that require replacing or refreshing at regular intervals. Mark your calendars to swap these items out on schedule:

- **Air filters:** Replace furnace, AC, and range hood filters every 1–3 months to improve efficiency.
- **Light bulbs:** Check interior and exterior bulbs monthly and replace burnt-out bulbs to maintain brightness.
- **Smoke detector batteries:** Replace smoke detector batteries twice a year at daylight savings time changes.
- **Water filters:** Replace sink, refrigerator, and whole home water filters every 6–12 months per manufacturer specs.
- **Fire extinguishers:** Inspect extinguishers monthly and replace every 6 years, or when pressure gauge is in the red.
- **Garbage-disposal blades:** Sharpen or replace disposal blades yearly to restore grinding performance.
- **Range-hood filters:** Clean grease off washable range hood filters monthly or replace disposable filters as needed.
- **HVAC tune-ups:** Have a technician perform a tune-up on heating and cooling equipment each year.
- **Septic tanks:** Have a professional pump out septic tanks every 3–5 years to prevent costly failures.

Seasonal Inspections and Repairs

Conduct thorough walkthrough inspections of your home and property during seasonal changes. Look for any signs of damage or required maintenance.

Spring

- Check the roof, siding, and windows for storm damage. Repair or replace damaged shingles, siding, cracked glass, and so on.
- Inspect the exterior for chipped paint and touch up as needed to protect from the elements.
- Clear out exterior drains and gutters clogged with leaves and debris over winter. Flush with a hose.
- Drain and service irrigation systems and lines before restarting for spring. Check for leaks.
- Open pool equipment and have a professional service and reopen the pool.

Summer

- Monitor exterior paint/stain, wood rot, moisture damage, pest activity, etc., and address as needed.
- Prune overgrown vegetation away from the home's exterior.
- Schedule HVAC tune-ups before peak cooling season.
- Monitor for musty smells signaling leaks or excess moisture, and immediately dry affected areas.

Fall

- Weatherproof doors, windows, pipes, and vents before winter—replace seals, caulk gaps, and install insulation.
- Winterize irrigation systems and lines—drain, blow out lines, and disconnect hoses.
- Winterize pools—drain, cover, and disconnect filtration and pumps.
- Schedule chimney cleaning and inspection before using fireplaces over the winter.

Winter

- Check attic for proper ventilation to avoid ice dams and moisture buildup.
- Inspect the roof and attic for critter activity and install screens, traps, or repellants as needed.
- Check insulation levels in the attic. Add insulation if below modern recommended R-values.

Ongoing Upkeep and Improvements

- Routinely check interior and exterior caulk and sealants around windows, doors, showers, sinks, and siding, and touch up or replace deteriorating caulk. Preventative sealing avoids major leaks.

- Keep up with small paint touch-ups on interior walls and exterior siding to keep everything looking fresh. Address scuffs and scrapes promptly.
- Inspect weather stripping around doors and windows and replace if worn to prevent drafts or water intrusion.
- Lubricate door hinges, locks, garage door tracks, etc., as needed to prevent binding and wear.
- Tighten loose screws, nails, and hardware; vibrations over time work them loose.
- Fix small issues like cracked tiles, warped boards, and wobbly railings before they worsen. Address problems early.

House-maintenance logs and notebooks tracking home info, warranties, and maintenance records in one spot simplifies staying on top of home ownership duties. Protect your largest investment through proper care.

Inspecting for Moisture Damage

Left unchecked, moisture from leaks, humidity, and condensation can cause extensive damage to structures and health hazards from mold growth:

- Monitor for bubbling paint and plaster or staining on walls or ceilings signaling a leak. Immediately dry affected areas.

- Look for moist windowsills, peeling exterior paint indicating condensation issues, or rotting wood.
- Note musty smells of mold/mildew and wet spots under sinks and behind appliances.
- Check bath exhaust fans are effectively venting humidity to prevent moisture buildup.
- Run a dehumidifier in problem rooms and fix sources of excess moisture like clogged drains under sinks.

Electrical System Maintenance

Electrical issues can quickly become fire hazards. Exercise diligence while performing maintenance:

- Check outlets for signs of overheating like scorch marks. Have an electrician upgrade wiring as needed.
- Ensure outdoor outlets are GFCI protected and enclosed in waterproof covers.
- Label circuit breakers clearly. Exercise breakers and ground fault interrupters monthly.
- Replace flickering light bulbs that signal wiring issues promptly.

Take Safety Precautions

Exercise proper precautions when undertaking maintenance tasks:

- Turn off power at the breaker panel and tag switches before electrical or plumbing work. Verify power is off.
- Use a voltage tester on wires before touching. Cap wires with wire nuts when disconnected.
- Keep fire extinguishers accessible in case of electrical or chemical mishaps.
- Back up and cap plumbing lines during repairs to prevent flooding.

Regularly maintaining your home helps maximize enjoyment of your living space while protecting functionality and property value. Being proactive with preventative care also makes home-ownership less stressful by averting crisis repairs. Keep your home in peak condition through diligent routine upkeep.

With preparation and a methodical approach, an array of home repairs can be tackled DIY, including drywall, flooring, fixtures, hardware, siding, and much more. While honing these skills takes time and practice, the payback is substantial through thousands saved in labor costs. And you can feel proud to pass down these practical abilities.

CONFIDENCE BUILDING OVER TIME

These are just a sampling of the many basic home repairs an amateur DIYer can successfully tackle. The key is building knowledge and proficiency over time. Don't hesitate to call in professional help whenever plumbing or electrical skills exceed your comfort zone.

Start by watching online repair tutorials to gain an understanding of the principles and steps involved before trying it yourself. Gather the necessary tools and materials beforehand. Work slowly with a focus on safety. Ask for assistance from more experienced friends when needed.

Learning home maintenance and DIY repair skills takes patience but pays dividends for years to come. You'll gain independence, valuable know-how, and confidence to handle situations as they arise. And nothing beats the pride and satisfaction of completing quality repairs yourself.

- **Proper planning prevents problems.** Analyzing the repair process, tools, and materials before starting prevents having to pause the project due to lack of preparation.
- **Organize your workspace.** Decluttering the workspace and preparing all necessary tools and materials within reach avoids wasting time searching midproject. This facilitates an organized, efficient workflow (Garskof, 2009).
- **Work in phases.** Tackling repairs in systematic phases —demolition, repair, cleaning, etc.—improves focus. Constantly shifting between tasks reduces productivity.
- **Enlist help when possible.** Having an extra set of hands speeds up repairs needing lifting, holding, and tight space access. Collaboration improves workflow.

- **Use the right tools.** Quality tools like power drills with adjustable speed settings provide more control and precision, preventing wasted effort on mistakes.
- **Take short breaks.** Short breaks improve mental clarity and stamina for working efficiently in focused bursts between periodic quick rests.
- **Invest in convenience upgrades.** Self-closing hinges and drawers reduce future maintenance time.

Proper planning, preparation, tools, and techniques significantly improve efficiency on DIY repairs, saving money and frustration. Work smarter, not harder.

CASE STUDY

James had always called a handyman for even minor repairs in his home, assuming he just "wasn't the handy type." But after moving into a new fixer-upper home with his girlfriend Emily, James knew he needed to start learning DIY maintenance skills to keep costs down.

The first project James attempted on his own was patching a few holes in the drywall. He studied a YouTube tutorial carefully, purchased the necessary supplies, and practiced on scrap drywall to get the technique right. Emily assisted with sanding and painting for a seamless finish.

Feeling empowered by his success, James moved on to bigger projects like replacing old plumbing fixtures and installing new interior doors throughout the home. He found that taking detailed notes and photos along the way helped refresh his memory each step of the process.

A year later, James feels capable of tackling any repair situation that arises, thanks to the DIY skills he has mastered. He saves money while also feeling a great sense of pride in caring for his home.

Now equipped with enhanced DIY competence, simple upgrades to our home's exterior bring immense curb-appeal returns while forging community connections.

Outdoor Projects and Curb Appeal

The exterior of your home shapes first impressions for visitors and neighbors. Investing sweat equity into improving outdoor spaces and curb appeal pays dividends in pride, functionality, and even neighborhood relationships. With proper planning and preparation, DIYers can take on rewarding projects to upgrade their home's exterior.

When deciding which projects to tackle, walk around your property through the eyes of a newcomer. Note areas that feel worn, dated, cluttered, or bare. Prioritize fixes that offer high visual impact like painting the front door a striking color or installing stylish house numbers (Family Handyman, 2019).

Functionality matters, too. Does the front walkway adequately light the way at night? Do you need more privacy or shade in the backyard? Address practical needs that improve usability along with aesthetics.

Curb-appeal projects need not be costly. Painting wooden features, pruning overgrown trees, or adding pretty planters can freshen up the look substantially. Take advantage of high-return investments like new welcome mats or house numbers.

Pay special attention to maintenance on home exteriors. Chipped paint, cobwebbed corners, and peeling walkways get magnified visually. Regular upkeep prevents costly repairs later (Consumer Affairs, 2023).

When undertaking larger upgrades, don't sacrifice quality to save money upfront. Using cheap materials on siding or decking will backfire. Invest for longevity.

Enhancing your home's exterior boosts neighborhood morale, too. Neighbors appreciate well-kept properties and may be inspired to improve their own landscaping or facades. A beautiful home exterior benefits the whole community.

IMPROVING OUTDOOR SPACES AND CURB APPEAL

The exterior of your home essentially extends your living space out into the surrounding neighborhood. The way you landscape, maintain, and decorate your outdoor areas greatly impacts not just functionality and aesthetics, but also relationships with nearby residents.

Jeff's experience highlights the importance of curb appeal. Shortly after moving into his new home, he hosted a neighborhood block party in his backyard. However, during the event he noticed most neighbors gravitating to front porches and back-yards of other homes instead of his own. Jeff realized he had neglected his exterior spaces, with an unfinished deck, patchy grass, weathered paint and trim, and lack of lighting or décor. To build stronger connections, he knew he needed to upgrade his home's curb appeal.

Some potential outdoor projects to consider include:

- landscaping with gardens, trees, plants, and eye-catching foliage.
- building a new deck or refinishing/restaining an existing deck or patio.
- updating exterior lighting fixtures by the front door, on patios, and along walkways.
- repainting or restaining faded siding, trim, railings, and other features.
- replacing a worn-out front door or dated garage door with more stylish options.
- installing an inviting front walkway from the driveway to the front entrance.
- adding exterior accents like planter boxes, benches, or potted plants.
- cleaning out and organizing worn outdoor storage sheds or spaces.

A few things to keep in mind when planning exterior improvements:

- Ensure proper drainage away from the home's foundation before landscaping.
- Use native plants well-suited for your region and specific sunlight exposure.
- Refresh old wood features like fences or benches by thoroughly sanding and applying new stain/sealer.
- Strategically group plants according to their soil, watering, and sunlight needs.
- Arrange exterior lighting to provide both ambiance for gatherings and safety along paths.

Transforming your home's outdoor curb appeal says you take pride in your home and want to positively contribute to the neighborhood landscape. A warm, tidy, and welcoming exterior subtly encourages neighbors to gather and forges community connections. Plus, you increase the long-term value and future sale appeal of your home.

Strategically placed landscaping like trees, shrubs, flowers, and foliage completely transforms plain exteriors into beautiful, welcoming spaces.

Consider these landscaping ideas:

- Plant fast-growing trees like crape myrtles to quickly add height, color, and shade.
- Contrast textures and colors, like pairing leafy hostas with crimson flowers.
- Build garden beds edged with stone or pavers for visual interest.

- Use landscaping to direct visitors to the main entrance.
- Add flowering pots, trellises, steppingstones, and other accents.
- Install a privacy fence or trees to define the property's borders.
- Use pea gravel or mulch to prevent mud in high-traffic areas.
- Group plants based on sunlight and water needs to simplify care.
- Illuminate landscaping with path lighting and spotlights.

Even novice DIYers can enhance their exterior through simple lawn care, planting attractive native flowers and shrubs, and adding a few eye-catching hardscape features.

LANDSCAPING FOR CURB APPEAL

Creating an appealing landscape with plants, trees, foliage, and hardscaping dramatically improves curb appeal while adding privacy.

Landscaping Tips

- Draw up designs mapping placement of plants, lighting, paths, and so on.
- Group plants with similar needs for efficient watering and care.

- Include native species naturally suited for the local climate and terrain.
- Add compost and fertilizer to nourish plants and soil.
- Edge and define beds with stones, bricks, or metal to keep tidy.
- Add hardscaping like paths, patios, or garden structures.
- Install irrigation with zones and timers for easy watering.
- Include decoration like outdoor art, sculpture, and water features.

Improving Curb Appeal

A home's curb appeal—its exterior appearance from the street—greatly impacts potential buyers' first impressions. There are many inexpensive ways to dramatically boost curb appeal. Some are listed here:

- **Landscaping:** Well-designed gardens, trees, plants, and foliage provide vibrant color while allowing homeowners to express personal style. This can increase a home's value by more than 20% (Family Handyman, 2019).
- **Exterior painting:** A fresh, modern exterior paint color coordinated with trim gives a facelift. Use quality primer and paint.

- **Outdoor lighting:** Path lighting guiding visitors to the front door provides both ambiance and safety. Update exterior fixtures.
- **Front door:** An updated, well-maintained front door with coordinating colors and hardware makes a bold statement.
- **Porch design:** An inviting front porch or seating area draws attention. Keep clutter free and add potted plants.
- **Garage doors:** Replace worn-out doors with stylish, updated carriage-house designs to transform the look.
- **Yard maintenance:** Well-manicured grass and neatly edged beds and walkways show pride of ownership.

With some sweat equity and strategic upgrades, you can utterly transform the exterior spaces to attract potential home buyers and improve relationships with neighbors (Liu, 2023). Curb appeal is about making your home inviting.

BUILDING DESIGNER DECKS AND PATIOS

Decks and patios extend outdoor living space and provide a surface for grilling, dining, and entertaining.

Keep the following in mind when planning deck and patio projects:

- Check permitting requirements for backyard structures.
- Ensure proper footings and support for safety and stability.
- Use weather-resistant decking like pressure treated lumber, composite, or PVC.
- Opt for low-maintenance materials like stone, pavers, or stamped concrete for patios.
- Incorporate built-in benches, planters, pergolas, or privacy screens.
- Include a fire pit, fireplace, or chiminea for ambiance.
- Add steps and railings conforming to local codes.
- Light the space for nighttime use with path illumination and overhead fixtures.
- Seal surfaces and use rugs to prevent slipping when wet.

Completing a full outdoor living space allows you to comfortably enjoy the backyard in any season.

Purpose of Decks and Patios

Decks and patios serve multiple important purposes for homeowners.

Expand Living Space

- Decks and patios effectively increase usable living area by bringing the indoors outdoors (Family Handyman, 2019).
- This added space allows for entertaining, dining, relaxing, playing, grilling, and hobbies.

Enhance Backyard Enjoyment

- Well-built decks and patios create an inviting outdoor oasis for everyday use (Garskof, 2009).
- Features like integrated benches, privacy screens, pergolas, and fire-pits extend functionality.

Increase Home Value

- Attractive decks and patios boost a home's value by providing additional living area for buyers (Liu, 2023).
- Outdoor enhancements are top renovations for return on investment upon home sale.

Foster Neighbor Relationships

- Inviting outdoor spaces provide an opportunity to comfortably host neighborhood gatherings (Lindsay, 2023).
- This facilitates stronger community connections.

With thoughtful design to maximize usability and aesthetics, decks and patios become invaluable additions that extend living space in a meaningful way while increasing home value. They become backyard destinations to enjoy for years to come.

DIY EXTERIOR UPGRADES

Beyond landscaping, several exterior upgrades can provide a big aesthetic impact without breaking the budget. A fresh coat of exterior paint works wonders. Power washing first improves adhesion. Use primer and high-quality paint.

Replace worn trim, shutters, railings, or columns with PVC or fiberglass for low maintenance. Swap dated entry doors and hardware for more modern styles that complement your home's look. Improve drab garage doors with updated modern carriage house designs and windows. Automate with smart openers. Repair and restain fences, decks, and other wood structures. Seal yearly.

Upgrade home numbers, mailbox, and porch lighting fixtures for a coordinated look.

Plant colorful annuals each season for vibrant curb appeal. Perennials return yearly.

Define property lines and obscure views with attractive trees or tall privacy hedges like arborvitae. Clean out rain gutters and wash siding. Trim overgrown bushes.

Maintain Appearance

With some DIY skills and planning, you can boost your home's exterior aesthetics without breaking the bank. Let neighbors take notice!

Outdoor DIY projects present opportunities to creatively express personality and style. Well-designed landscaping or an inviting front porch reflect the homeowner's preferences. Neighbors take interest and pride in an improved home exterior.

Exterior upgrades foster stronger neighborhood connections by providing welcoming spaces to comfortably interact and socialize outside. Improving the outside appearance shows that homeowners care about the community aesthetic.

With the right motivation, tools, and budget, both novice and experienced DIYers can successfully take on projects to boost curb appeal and forge community bonds. The tangible and intangible returns make home exterior upgrades extremely worthwhile.

In summary, exterior improvements not only increase financial value but also provide creative outlets for homeowners to leave a positive mark on the neighborhood landscape while facilitating relationships. The benefits inside and out make DIY exterior projects a vital investment.

CASE STUDY: LINDA'S CURB-APPEAL MAKEOVER

Linda was embarrassed by the state of her home's exterior, with faded siding, overgrown landscaping, and a splintering deck and fence past their prime. She wanted to create an outdoor space welcoming to neighbors and reflective of her bright and cheerful personality.

She started by power washing the siding and deck to remove grime before restaining. Flower beds were cleared of weeds and edged with stone borders. A new cedar pergola provided structure within a fresh garden layout.

The worn front door and dingy garage door were replaced with bold, cheerful colors complemented by modern exterior lighting. Linda finished off with colorful potted annuals flanking the front entry.

"I feel like I have a brand-new home that I now love to share with neighbors and friends," Linda said. "The joy I get from my beautiful outdoor oasis is worth every penny and minute spent."

Linda's thoughtful improvements turned her home into the most popular on the block for gatherings. Her personalized touches sparked similar upgrades throughout the neighborhood.

The exterior of a home makes the all-important first impression. Investing DIY time and budget into your outdoor spaces pays dividends through increased home value, improved relationships with neighbors, and years of enjoyment.

With imagination and elbow grease, you can utterly transform the landscaping, hardscaping, lighting, and architectural details that elevate your home from forgettable to the envy of the neighborhood. Curb appeal begins at the curb but extends into a welcoming backyard oasis.

DIY Skills for Dads

For fathers with packed schedules, learning DIY skills may feel daunting. But equipping yourself with practical fix-it know-how allows saving time and money while modeling self-reliance for your kids. Follow these tips to develop essential home improvement capabilities amidst the demands of fatherhood.

Start by identifying the most urgent needs in your living space. Does the faucet leak? Are cabinets loose? Address glaring issues first to build confidence. Children notice improvements, and it keeps Mom happy!

Gather the core tools suited for common tasks like hanging photos, assembling furniture, patching walls, and basic installations. Quality over quantity prevents frustration. Build your toolkit gradually as skills improve (This Old House, 2010).

When tackling repairs, review manufacturer instructions thoroughly and watch online how-to videos. Pausing tutorials while you work enables mimicking techniques. Troubleshoot problems methodically before calling a professional (DIY Daddy, 2019).

Schedule focused regular time slots for projects by capitalizing on nap times or free weekends. Split bigger efforts into stages. Milestones maintain momentum and make tasks feel manageable.

Involve kids in age-appropriate ways to foster shared learning. Let them help fetch tools or hold materials in place. Descriptively narrate steps being taken to explain the skills. Praise their assistance.

Resist perfectionism. Don't let small missteps undermine confidence and derail progress. Mistakes happen during learning. Celebrate getting fixes done over flawless finishes.

Patience and persistence pay off. Few develop DIY skills overnight. But consistent practice together with a spirit of creative problem solving will enable you to tackle more repairs successfully over time.

Mastering basic DIY empowers dads to contribute meaningfully while saving money. And nothing builds children's admiration more than seeing Dad competently install a new light fixture or patch a hole in the wall!

TEACHING DIY SKILLS TO CHILDREN

A startling 85% of fathers do not actively make an effort to teach DIY and home improvement skills to their children (This Old House, 2010). However, dads who intentionally make it a priority to share their hard-earned expertise provide invaluable lessons for life, strengthen family bonds, and create meaningful intergenerational connections.

Hands-on learning sticks with kids far more than conceptual instruction alone. Teaching children practical DIY skills from a young age has many benefits beyond preparing them for future repairs. Teaching children:

- develops independence, confidence, self-reliance, and perseverance.
- promotes fine motor skills, spatial reasoning, and creative problem solving.
- provides an engaging outlet for active, kinetic learning.
- encourages safety awareness, responsibility, and preparedness.
- establishes a shared hobby and opportunities for quality bonding.
- gives kids an immense sense of pride and accomplishment in their abilities.
- sets children up with essential, practical life skills for adulthood.

With proper adult supervision, kids as young as 3–5 can start gaining competence with manageable tasks like using child-safe hand tools, planting seeds, or assembling structures from blocks. Safety should always be the top priority. But with some patience and planning, teaching DIY skills can become a beloved family tradition.

PLANNING AGE-APPROPRIATE PROJECTS

Making DIY an engaging experience for young kids requires age-appropriate planning and hands-on involvement. Consider these tips when getting started:

- Let kids actively assist with tasks and tools suitable for their developmental skill level. Provide help as needed.
- Start with small, simple DIY projects using child-safe materials and hand tools. Don't overwhelm them early on.
- Celebrate small successes like hanging a picture, planting a seed, or assembling blocks. This builds motivation and self-esteem.
- Designate a kids' workspace for projects to keep their focus without clutter and distractions.
- Closely supervise all tasks, repeatedly demonstrating safe tool usage and habits. Don't leave them unattended.
- Find unique projects that align with your child's interests, like making jewelry, race cars, bird houses, etc., to maximize engagement.
- Encourage creativity by letting them decorate their finished projects with paint, stickers, and glitter.

- Ask questions throughout the process to evaluate comprehension and support critical thinking.
- Take frequent breaks to maintain safety and focus when attention spans drift. Learning takes mental energy.
- End each lesson on a high note after successfully completing an engaging step. Don't drag on past exhaustion.

Passing Down a Love for DIY

More than merely preparing kids for future DIY projects, sharing these skills is about passing down a love for building, working with your hands, and problem solving. Kids cherish the feeling of collaborating on projects alongside parents and grandparents. The whole experience builds family bonds and memories, not just the finished products.

Safety habits established young stick for life. But the hands-on competence, independence, focus, planning abilities, and pride of achievement learned carry far beyond individual projects. DIY becomes part of their identity.

Starting young develops enthusiasm and curiosity around home improvement, wood/tool crafts, gardening, electronics, vehicle maintenance, and other hands-on hobbies kids can pursue for decades to come. Passing down specialized skills, techniques, and wisdoms equips the next generation, but also connects families across generations.

FOSTERING HOME IMPROVEMENT SKILLS IN KIDS

Fathers play a crucial role in passing down cherished DIY knowledge and skills to their children. Studies show that more than 90% of men learned home improvement skills from their dads and grandfathers (This Old House, 2010). However, alarmingly, only 50% have taken proactive steps to teach their own children those invaluable hands-on abilities.

Making DIY education a priority in the formative years provides enormous benefits for kids that last a lifetime. Hands-on learning sticks with children in a deeper way than conceptual instruction alone. Teaching DIY skills through demonstration, participation, and guidance builds practical competence, confidence, independence, and an eagerness to help around the house. Starting young plants the seed that can grow into a life-long passion.

Safety First

As with any hands-on learning, safety should be the number-one priority. Take time to instill proper habits and respect around tool usage from an early age. Ensure kids wear appropriate protective gear like closed-toe shoes, gloves, and goggles. Carefully demonstrate correct grips and techniques before letting them try. Always provide close adult supervision when tools are in use. Don't allow operation of potentially dangerous tools like saws until kids are older and show sufficient maturity and dexterity to handle them responsibly.

Cover Age-Appropriate Safety Procedures Before Embarking on any Project

Following is a list of safety topics to cover with your child:

- Review tool handling, weight, sharp points, pinch hazards, and more.
- Discuss electrical dangers and avoiding outlets/cords.
- Explain kickback risks with saws.
- Stress wearing eye and ear protection.
- Caution about falling objects and head protection.
- Teach proper lifting form to avoid back injuries.
- Install GFCI outlets and circuit breakers.
- Keep a well-stocked first aid kit accessible.
- Monitor for fatigue and have kids take breaks as needed.

Start with manageable tasks that minimize risk, like using a screwdriver or sandpaper. Provide guidance but foster independence appropriate for their skill level. With common-sense precautions, kids can learn to safely handle tools at any age under watchful parental supervision.

Building Confidence and Competence

Starting kids on DIY projects at a young age helps build the confidence and competence needed to successfully take on more complex improvements as they get older. But beyond merely preparing them for future work, it also teaches problem-solving abilities, perseverance, spatial reasoning, creativity, planning, math, and other academic and life skills.

The sense of accomplishment kids gain from seeing their hard work result in a completed project is extremely rewarding. Give them an active role in the process with age—appropriate tasks rather than just having them watch passively. Offer frequent encouragement and celebratory high fives along the way. Mastering even the most basic skills makes kids beam with pride and eagerness to continue learning.

The optimal projects provide just enough challenge to build emerging skills without overwhelming kids' capabilities. Be flexible—if interest is waning, switch gears to maintain engagement. Encourage them to decorate finished projects to build creativity.

Fostering Excitement

Injecting an element of playfulness and healthy competition can get kids genuinely enthusiastic about DIY. For example, challenge them to:

- have fastener driving contests using a hammer and nails.
- compete to stack blocks or domino's the highest before toppling.
- race to assemble jigsaw puzzles or snap circuits fastest.

- organize a workspace relay, retrieving tools one at a time.
- bury and uncover plastic eggs packed with candy in the dirt.
- play hide-and-seek around project materials and tools.

The goal is to get them intrinsically motivated by making it exhilarating. Create special family rituals and inside jokes associated with the work. Any task, even tedious ones like sanding or sweeping, can be infused with fun incentives. Their eagerness will make them more attentive, engaged learners.

Bonding Through Projects

Hands down, the most significant long-term benefit of teaching DIY skills is the intergenerational bonding it facilitates. By mentoring kids through home projects, fathers build treasured memories together and pass down specialized knowledge honed over their lifetime. Kids cherish the traditions, inside tips, rituals, and stories acquired together in the midst of the sawdust.

The lessons connect generations through a common culture and language. Kids often gravitate back to these abilities as teens and young adults, occasionally even teaching Dad some new tricks. DIY becomes encoded in the family identity.

Turn chores into opportunities for meaningful mentorship. Explain how best to use tools and why techniques matter while you work together. Share funny stories of past mishaps and accomplishments. Take pride in a job well done side by side. Kids will remember the time spent creating something meaningful together.

With patience, care, and creativity, dads can instill a lifelong passion and skillset for home improvement in their children. Teaching practical DIY abilities not only saves money over hiring contractors later in life but, more importantly, connects families through generations of shared knowledge, meaningful mentoring, and lasting memories.

DEVELOPMENTAL BENEFITS OF INTRODUCING DIY SKILLS TO CHILDREN

Children develop rapidly across physical, cognitive, and emotional domains in the first 5–6 years of life. Early introduction to DIY skills and hands-on projects can provide huge benefits tailored to their formative stages. Hands-on learning sticks with kids, imparting confidence, knowledge, and passion for home improvement.

Ages 3–4

At ages 3–4, children have very limited attention spans but learn quickly through sensory interaction. Introduce basic hand tool use like screw drivers or hammers with close parental supervision. Simple sensory DIY projects keep them engaged while developing hand-eye coordination, such as:

- decorating flowerpots or picture frames with glitter, paint, stickers, and other fun crafty items.
- hammering golf tees into Styrofoam to make shapes and patterns.
- screwing nuts onto bolts held securely by parents.
- gluing popsicle sticks to make shapes.

Go at their pace and keep sessions brief. Praise their accomplishments and involvement. Ensure proper safety gear like gloves and goggles.

Age 5

By age 5, focus and attention span increase, allowing participation in slightly more complex projects with assistance. Key developmental benefits include:

- following step-by-step instructions to complete a project.
- learning to use child-safe hand tools with guidance.
- accomplishing goals through persistence and effort.

- fostering creativity by decorating their completed projects.
- developing focus by working at a task from start to finish.

Fun introductory projects include making birdhouses, toolboxes, race cars, jewelry, and other crafts with parental supervision. Let them get creative decorating their accomplishments.

Ages 6–7

At ages 6–7, comprehension skills allow kids to take on more multistep projects by:

- following illustrated instructions for a build process.
- accurately measuring and marking materials needed for projects.
- safely handling hammers, wrenches, screwdrivers, and other hand tools.
- assisting with project steps like drilling pilot holes.
- using basic math and fractions for measurement.
- crafting more elaborate items like model airplanes.

Emphasize safety procedures and technique while fostering independence. DIY teaches perseverance through completing longer projects.

Ages 8–10

From ages 8–10, attention spans lengthen significantly. Kids also gain strength and stamina. By this stage, most can:

- work on DIY projects for an hour, or longer, with some breaks.
- comprehend and follow multistep written instructions.
- accurately measure materials and make cuts assisted by parents.
- use hand tools proficiently with training on proper techniques.
- assist with operating power tools like drills while supervised.
- complete more complex crafts and builds semi-independently.

Emphasize safety procedures when introducing tools. Parental guidance is still needed for more difficult steps. DIY builds their sense of accomplishment.

Ages 10–12

By ages 10–12, kids experience major cognitive and physical advancements. Their capabilities include:

- performing project steps independently with instructions and supervision.
- using hand and power tools proficiently after training.

- increased safety awareness when handling tools.
- the ability to make measurements, cuts, and alterations to project plans as needed.
- focus to complete multihour building projects over days with guidance.
- handling moderately complex builds like furniture, outdoor structures, and others.

With proper adult supervision, most kids this age can use power tools like circular saws, jigsaws, and drills. Stress the responsibility that tool usage entails. Foster their growing independence and pride.

By gradually introducing DIY skills tailored to their developmental stage, kids gain confidence, knowledge, safety awareness, perseverance, focus, and passion for home improvement. The hands-on learning sticks with them and lays a foundation for tackling their own projects one day as adults.

Tips for Maximizing Developmental Benefits

- Start young, around ages 3–4, with highly supervised simple tasks.
- Tailor projects to align with cognitive and physical abilities at each age.
- Ensure proper safety gear, like gloves, goggles, and closed-toe shoes.
- Demonstrate proper tool usage and techniques before letting them try.
- Don't leave them unattended when tools are in use.

- Assist with any dangerous steps requiring cutting or power tools.
- Break projects into stages appropriate for their attention span.
- Offer frequent encouragement and praise their effort and involvement.
- Let them decorate their projects to foster creativity and pride.
- Tie in math by measuring materials together.
- Adjust plans as needed based on their skills and engagement.
- Keep it fun with humor; laugh at mistakes to lighten perfectionism.

DIY projects make cherished memories while teaching invaluable life skills. As the adult, you provide the supervision and guidance needed to ensure these hands-on learning experiences are safe, educational, and fulfilling.

MAKING DIY FUN FOR KIDS

If you want the DIY experience with your kids to be rewarding, rather than frustrating, you will need patience and creativity. The key is making the learning process engaging and tailored to their developing abilities.

Consider these tips to help ensure success.

Let kids Choose Fun Projects That Interest Them

Rather than rigidly assigning tasks, allow kids to select DIY projects that genuinely interest them. Making birdhouses for neighborhood birds or race cars to run along tracks are far more intriguing than being told to sand a board or organize tools. Their excitement will make them more attentive and focused learners.

Break Tasks Down Into Simple, Achievable Steps

Chunk down projects into discrete, achievable steps appropriate for their skill level. Cut materials ahead of time. Predrill any holes. Demonstrate single skills needed, like how to use a paintbrush. Having a clear roadmap to follow prevents being overwhelmed. Celebrate conquering each milestone along the way.

Use Vibrant Tools and Materials That Capture Their Attention

Opt for paint colors, hardware, fabrics, and materials in their favorite bright hues. Let them get creative combining items. For example, mix different-colored screws on a project. The hands-on learning sticks better when they are fully engaged with tactile, visual, and sensory input.

Take Lots of Breaks to Reset When Focus Drifts

Due to kids' short attention spans, regularly stop for water, snack, or stretching breaks. Switch up activities if restlessness persists. Short bursts of focused work maximize learning retention at this age over prolonged projects. End on a high note rather than dragging on beyond exhaustion.

Make Lessons Interactive and Tactile

Set lessons to songs or create engaging mnemonic chants. Paint a mural demonstrating tool safety. Plant seeds in sensory bins filled with dirt, seeds, and gardening tools. Kinetic learning through play makes abstract concepts concrete.

Ensure Proper Safety Gear Is Sized to Fit Comfortably

Ill-fitting goggles, gloves, ear protection, and other PPE is uncomfortable and likely to be disregarded. Invest in kids' versions of essential safety equipment. Try different styles until you find options they don't mind wearing. This builds healthy lifelong habits.

End Sessions on a High Note Before Fatigue Sets In

Once distraction or frustration arises, it's best to wind down DIY time for the day. Whether an hour or 10 minutes, finish up after successful completion of a meaningful step they can feel proud of. This motivates them to want to continue next time.

Recognize Effort and Share in the Victory

More than the final product, emphasize the effort involved at their age level. Offer enthusiastic high fives for focus, trying a new tool, problem solving, or listening to safety rules. Celebrate the intrinsic joys and accomplishments of building rather than just the end result.

With creativity, patience, and engagement tailored their developing abilities, DIY time can become a beloved bonding tradition. Creating positive experiences builds enthusiasm for learning invaluable practical life skills.

Key Parenting Strategies for Fostering DIY in Kids

Set Clear Expectations for Behavior and Responsibility

Establish ground rules for conduct like "no horseplay with tools" or "no wandering off midproject." Reinforce responsibility for following safety protocols. Guidelines create a productive learning environment.

Explain Tool Usage Before Starting

Walk through how each DIY tool is held and handled prior to letting them try. Share tips only adults know from experience. Verbal instruction paired with demonstration prevents fumbling.

Ensure Your Workspace Is Clutter-Free

Declutter project areas to minimize distractions for their developing focus. Keep walkways clear to avoid tripping hazards.

Organize materials needed nearby but out of the main work zone.

Demonstrate Proper Techniques Step-By-Step

Break down each new DIY skill like sanding, drilling or nailing into individual steps shown slowly first. Mimic your motions verbally and with hand-over-hand guidance. Mastery requires understanding the subskills.

Help Them Draw Project Plans

Having them sketch a project plan gets them invested in the process while building visualization abilities. Assist converting plans into usable outlines. Planning clarifies objectives and materials required.

Highlight PPE Importance for Injury Prevention

Emphasize how proper gear like goggles, gloves, and closed-toe shoes prevents injuries before they happen. Share real stories of avoiding harm thanks to safety habits. Make wearing them an essential job responsibility.

Guide Hands-On to Avoid Mistakes

Rather than verbal directions alone, guide them physically through new skills until techniques are instilled. Prevent frustration and safety risks from potentially dangerous mistakes made when unsupervised.

Ask Engaging Questions Throughout

Keep them focused by consistently asking engaging questions about next steps, tool choices, safety considerations, or anything else you're working on. Check comprehension periodically. Stimulate their thinking.

Praise Effort, Persistence, and Asking for Help

More than outcomes, recognize diligence, focus, and willingness to try challenging tasks, asking questions, and requesting help when needed. These traits make proficient lifelong DIYers.

Celebrate Pride in Accomplishments

Mark progress with ceremony whether a mini-ribbon-cutting or round of applause. Give genuine praise for completed projects to feed intrinsic motivation. Help them confidently exclaim, "I built that!"

With commitment to positive educational experiences, DIY projects can become beloved bonding traditions, building character while imparting practical skills benefitting kids for life.

CASE STUDY: MIKE'S GARAGE WORKSHOP WITH KIDS

Mike grew up working with his dad on home improvement tasks and hoped to continue the tradition with his own children. When his twin boys turned 5, Mike decided the time was right to get them involved with DIY.

He cleaned up half of his cluttered garage to create a kid-friendly workspace. They picked out child-sized safety gear together. For their first project, Mike guided them through building a simple birdhouse kit.

Over the next few years, the boys learned to use hand tools safely with supervision and to make increasingly complex projects. By ages 8–9, they used power drills, sanders, and even basic saws under Mike's watchful eye.

Now teenagers, Mike's sons have built bookshelves, picnic tables, and many other creations in the family's special garage workshop, thanks to their dad's patience and guidance. The experience bonded them through shared skills and accomplishments.

One day, while working on a new project, Mike paused to watch his sons collaborate. He was filled with pride at the competent, caring young men they had become. But he also felt a twinge of sadness, realizing their childhood days in the workshop were numbered as they grew more independent.

Mike treasured these final memories even more, knowing the boys would soon move on to studies, careers, and families of their own. Though bittersweet, he found comfort knowing the problem-solving skills and work ethic they developed together would serve them well in life. For now, Mike cherished each precious moment remaining as they worked side-by-side.

Celebrating Success and Future Projects

Upon completing a challenging DIY project, it's important to pause and celebrate your accomplishment before quickly moving on to the next item on your home improvement to-do list. Properly acknowledging successes maintains motivation and energy for future endeavors.

Start by examining the finished project with a sense of pride. Note specific elements you handled well, like perfect tile seams, crisp paint lines, or a creatively solved problem. Recognize the new skills you've developed in the process.

Share photos of the completed project with family and friends. Let them express congratulations and admiration for your work. This external validation helps cement your sense of achievement.

Evaluate ways you can build upon the lessons learned to improve efficiency or quality next time. Think through what supplies, tools, or knowledge would have made aspects easier. Improving your process is an ongoing endeavor.

Take time to thoroughly clean your work area and return tools to their designated spots. This provides closure to the project and readiness for the next. Decluttering enables starting fresh.

Enjoy the functional improvements and aesthetic upgrades your effort accomplished. Soak in the satisfaction of having created an enhancement to your living space with your own hands.

Discuss potential future projects together with your partner, children, or roommates. Collaboratively choose the next most meaningful effort to tackle.

Periodically repeat any needed maintenance on past upgrades like recaulking or restaining. Your past successes will reward you long term with proper upkeep.

By celebrating accomplishments before rushing ahead, you reinforce pride, confidence, and enthusiasm for DIY projects. And thoughtfully planning future efforts keeps the positive momentum going.

REFLECTING ON ACCOMPLISHMENTS

After months, or even years, of completing DIY and home improvement projects together, it's important for couples to pause and reflect on the journey so far. Much like building Rome, enhancing your living space and relationship takes time, happening incrementally with each task completed.

Take a moment to review what you've accomplished:

- Walk through each room, noting all the upgrades and transformations—fresh paint colors, new lighting fixtures, refinished floors, and more. Appreciate the ambiance you've created.
- Look back at old photos and videos to see how far you've come. Reminisce over the outdated styles you've updated for modern eras.
- Review your original Honey Do list, checking off finished projects. Take pride in how many items have been systematically crossed off the list through teamwork.
- Make a list of all the new skills you've developed, like tiling, drywall repair, appliance installation, and finishing work. Consider how empowered this makes you feel.
- Calculate potential savings over hiring contractors for all your projects. One study found DIYers save $330 per project on average (This Old House, 2023). That adds up fast!
- Identify your proudest achievements and the biggest challenges you've overcome. Maybe it was remodeling a bathroom solo or learning to install a new stair railing together.
- Ask your partner for feedback on your biggest successes. What transformations are they most proud of? What moments stood out?
- Give yourself credit for pushing through frustrations

and obstacles along the way. Not everything went smoothly, but you persisted.

- Appreciate how this shared experience has brought you closer through communication, compromise, and seeing each other's creative talents shine.

- Consider hosting a party or an open house to show off finished projects to family and neighbors. Celebrate all the blood, sweat, and tears.

With reflection often comes motivation to keep the momentum going.

Set New Goals

- Brainstorm fresh projects based on current needs and interests. Prioritize updates that will improve daily life.

- Stretch your abilities to build additional skills, like learning tiling after mastering painting. Growth takes focus.

- Involve kids in projects to foster their self-confidence while passing down the DIY mindset. Make it a family tradition.

- Plan outdoor living-space enhancements as seasons change. Warm weather opens new doors.

- Help neighbors with projects after mastering them yourself. Pay it forward in your community.

- Maintain your home through routine seasonal care and upkeep. A little prevention goes far.

No matter where you are in the process, be proud of all you've accomplished! The Honey Do list is a lifelong journey, not a destination. There's always more to do, but consistent progress leads to amazing results over time. Pausing to reflect reconnects you with the joy of creating a home and future memories together.

Additional Ideas to Consider

- Make a commemorative sign or art piece honoring your most meaningful projects.
- Have a plaque made, engraved with your names and the year your biggest project was completed.
- Start a DIY journal detailing your projects, lessons learned, mishaps, and accomplishments.
- Frame inspiring photos from your projects to display in your newly upgraded rooms.
- Have a movie night and pull up old footage from projects you can now look back on and laugh.
- Research your home's history, construction year, and previous owners. Appreciate renovations over the decades.
- Re-create old family photos in updated rooms to highlight striking before and after contrasts.
- Interview each other on camera reflecting on your proudest moments, struggles, and memories.
- Compile an album or digital collection of project photos to pass down for generations.

- Write encouraging notes about your partner's growth throughout this experience.

The Honey Do list brought you closer in so many ways. Take time to genuinely reflect on the blood, sweat, tears, and laughter that went into enhancing your home and relationship. Celebrate each other for what you've achieved together. And remember—the adventure continues one new project at a time!

THE TRANSFORMATIVE POWER OF REFLECTION

Reflection plays a vital role in extracting lessons from the DIY experience. Taking time to reflect:

- provides perspective on how far you've come as a couple and individuals.
- allows you to clearly articulate the specific skills you've gained.
- reveals areas of strength to build on and weaknesses to refine.
- motivates you by amplifying wins, milestones, and accomplishments.
- lets you pause and process amidst the busyness of projects.
- fosters gratitude for teamwork with your partner.
- helps identify next goals and new opportunities.

Reflection is most powerful when shared together as a couple. Verbalizing thoughts and emotions helps crystallize practical learnings, meaningful memories, sources of pride, and insights into your relationship. You'll likely deepen intimacy as you discover mutual takeaways from the experience.

Set time quarterly or annually to intentionally reflect on key topics:

- **Favorite project memories:** Share specific moments that brought you joy, laughter, fulfillment, or a sense of accomplishment and pride. Reconnect with the meaning behind the work.
- **New skills:** Appreciate practical abilities gained like tiling, woodwork, electrical, and plumbing. Discuss how these new confidence levels make you feel.
- **Overcoming obstacles:** Talk through frustrations you faced and important lessons learned from mistakes or mishaps. Find the growth opportunities.
- **Home transformation:** Pinpoint visible upgrades room by room. Share your favorite renovations and appreciations of each other's talents.
- **Partnership growth:** Consider specific ways collaboration strengthened your communication, compromise, trust, and bond.
- **Future dreams:** Brainstorm and get excited about next projects and possibilities. Reflecting fuels motivation.

Additional Reflective Questions to Explore Together

- What project or moment are you most proud of and why?

- What funny memories or inside jokes were created along the way?
- How did you each support the other through challenges or frustrations?
- What part of the home's transformation brought you the most joy?
- How did you balance each other's ideas, talents, and priorities?
- Which new skills are you most eager to learn next?
- What lessons about teamwork did you learn?
- How did the experience deepen your relationship?
- What wisdom could you pass on to others embarking on DIY journeys?
- How did the Honey Do list change your outlook on home projects?
- What inspired you about watching your partner discover new capabilities?
- How has your confidence evolved?
- What memories will you cherish decades from now?

The simple act of periodic reflection together catalyzes fresh motivation, insights, and growth. It provides perspective on the deeper meaning behind the nuts-and-bolts projects and power of doing them alongside your partner.

Here are some ideas for optimizing meaningful reflection together:

- Schedule reflection sessions like you would a project. Protect the time.
- Set a comfortable, relaxing mood—light candles, pour a glass of wine, put on music.
- Print photos from projects to stir memories as you reflect.
- Alternate sharing, being present, and actively listening without judgement.
- Jot down notes to crystallize learnings and aspirations.
- Appreciate vulnerabilities and emotions that surface.
- End with a renewed sense of purpose and direction.
- Reflect consistently before, during, and after projects —not just at the end.
- Consider informal reflections while driving or strolling together.
- Use a journal to capture ongoing individual insights. Share entries.

Thoughtful reflection provides the indispensable gift of perspective—both on the tangible home improvements achieved and the intangible gains for your relationship beneath the surface. Renew motivation by regularly reviewing the proud milestones in your rearview mirror while also discussing hopes on the road ahead. Keep growing together.

THOUGHTFUL WAYS TO REFLECT

Here are some meaningful exercises and activities to guide reflective discussion and fully appreciate your DIY journey:

- Slowly stroll through each room, admiring the upgrades and transformations together. Appreciate the ambiance you've created.
- Recall special memories tied to projects in each space. Let the emotions and nostalgia surface.
- Note the ways, both large and subtle, that your home feels fresh, functional, and tailored to your family.
- Gather old photos taken before renovations began in each area. Compare to current photos.
- Discuss the outdated styles, worn finishes, and inefficient layouts you've updated for modern eras and needs.
- Appreciate the striking transformations side-by-side. Feel proud of the vision brought to life.
- Laugh together over decor choices that seemed stylish then but make you cringe now.
- Dig up those early scribbled to-do lists, Honey Do lists, renovations plans, and DIY notes.
- Review the timeline and progress for each project. Discuss key milestones and breakthroughs.
- Appreciate early ideas that evolved for the better with experience. Value lessons learned.
- Get a sense of accomplishment seeing all targeting planning transformed into reality.

- Re-create your original DIY and Honey Do lists. Review and check off each task done.
- Estimate the dollar value saved doing projects yourself versus hiring contractors.
- Discuss the most tedious items or physically demanding jobs. Appreciate persevering together.
- Pick favorite completed projects that brought a sense of fulfillment and pride.
- Share specific ways your communication, compromise, and trust grew through this teamwork.
- Appreciate how you balanced each other's ideas, strengths, and preferences.
- Note areas for improvement in partnership as future projects continue.
- Verbalize how your appreciation and admiration for each other has deepened.
- Offer genuine praise and thanks for your partner's efforts, from planning to working to encouragement.
- Discuss the role each person played and virtues displayed like persistence, creativity, and positivity.
- Appreciate the sacrifices made by both parties to create something meaningful.
- Leave sticky notes around the house praising each other's accomplishments and talents shown.
- Place loving notes concealed in projects to be discovered and reread years later, during renovations.
- Frame a collaborative thank-you letter noting memorable moments and expressing excitement about the future together.

- Record an oral history interview reminiscing favorite memories and reflecting on lessons learned.
- Make a commemorative sign, plaque, or art piece noting major projects completed together.
- Have a plaque engraved with your names and the year your biggest renovation was completed.
- Create a DIY time capsule of project photos and memorabilia to open years later.
- Bake a celebratory cake or favorite home-cooked meal together to enjoy as you reflect.
- Create a digital photo album or video set to music that captures your journey.

Leveraging reflection to celebrate shared accomplishments will amplify the pride, confidence, and connection derived from home improvement achievements. Reflection provides perspective on what the projects represent—an investment into your living space and relationship. Commit to reflect thoughtfully and often.

SETTING FUTURE GOALS

Reflection on your DIY journey so far also fuels motivation to keep your home improvement momentum going strong. Take time to brainstorm and get excited about future project ideas together. Possibilities are listed next.

Add New Features Based on Evolving Family Needs

As your family grows and changes over the years, so will your needs from your living space. Brainstorm ways to proactively make adaptations for anticipated lifestyle shifts. If you have a baby on the way, plan safety upgrades like rounded corners on furniture and outlet covers. If the kids are nearing college, discuss converting bedrooms to new uses like a home office, when they leave the nest. Downsizing in retirement? Look for ways to increase accessibility and convenience.

Develop Skills Together in New Areas

Make a list of home improvement skills you each want to develop next, such as tiling, electrical work, or installing wood floors. Learning together expands your joint capabilities while being enjoyable. Build on your core competencies by taking on projects to gain proficiency in 1–2 new areas annually. Sign up for courses at your local home improvement store.

Embark on the Next Phase of Renovations Room-By-Room

Create a master checklist of remaining renovations desired in each room. Prioritize these by necessity, cost, and effort. Spread out major overhauls over time, moving systematically from one space to the next to balance out the workload. Carry the fresh style elements from your earlier rooms into the new areas.

Plan Outdoor Living-Space Enhancements Across Seasons

Dream up exciting ways to further enhance your exterior spaces to be enjoyed across seasons. Build a fire pit for cooler months. Install a water feature or shady pergola for hot summer days in the yard. Strategically add landscaping and foliage suited for different times of the year.

Organize and Simplify Existing Spaces

Declutter over-stuffed areas and build custom storage solutions to maximize function of your current layouts. Incorporate space-saving tips from home organization experts to reduce belongings while maintaining utility. Simplify what you own to just the essentials.

Maintain Improvements Through Diligent Cleaning and Upkeep

Create master lists of routine maintenance required for your home improvements, such as annual sealing of floors and deck, gutter cleaning, filter changes, touch-up painting, and much, much more. Schedule time every month to performs a task like checking smoke detectors, inspecting the roof, and cleaning window treatments. Preventative care preserves your hard work.

Create a Vision Board

Gather inspiring photos, fabric swatches, and sketches representing your shared hopes for future renovations. Collaboratively make a vision board showcasing the projects and upgrades you want to complete in the next 1, 5, and 10 years. Verbalize your motivations and come to a consensus on priorities. Visualizing the possibilities together makes them feel more tangible as you chart the road ahead.

Balance New Complex Projects With Quick Wins

To sustain steady progress, balance larger renovations with quick maintenance tasks and upgrades. Swap out all sink fixtures and shower heads one weekend for a visible transformation through minimal effort. Clean and freshen paint between major projects. Blending ambitious endeavors with simple quick hits provides variety and continual enhancement.

The DIY and home improvement journey is a lifelong process rather than a single destination. Regular reflection, thoughtful goal-setting, and diligent home maintenance keeps you moving forward as a team. Revisit and evolve your home vision as needs change. But always protect time for open communication and celebrating wins—both big and small—together.

CASE STUDY: TODD AND HEATHER'S DIY JOURNEY

When Todd first received the lengthy Honey Do list from his wife, Heather, he felt totally overwhelmed and unprepared. But Heather's encouragement inspired Todd to methodically develop his DIY skills over time.

Years later, the couple finally paused to reflect on their home improvement journey. They laughed looking back at photos of the bland "before" rooms they'd transformed through teamwork.

"Our master bedroom overhaul was my proudest moment," said Heather. "Seeing Todd's confidence grow throughout that project was so rewarding."

They also discussed frustrations like when their lack of tiling experience resulted in having to redo the kitchen backsplash. "We sure learned a lot from our mistakes, too," Todd chuckled.

Moving forward, Heather and Todd set new goals, like remodeling the kids' bathroom and building an outdoor kitchen. They felt eager to tackle future projects together.

"Reflecting on how far we've come as a couple through this journey motivates us to keep taking on new challenges," Heather added.

Keeping the Game Alive

Now that you have everything you need to master DIY, it's time to pass on your newfound knowledge and guide other readers on their DIY journey.

By leaving your honest opinion of "The Honey Do List For Guys DIY Made Easy" on Amazon, you'll not only help fellow DIYers find the information they seek but also ignite their passion for DIY.

Thank you for your help. The DIY community thrives when we share our knowledge – and you're helping us do just that.

Scan the QR code to leave your review on Amazon.

Conclusion

We've now reached the end of our journey together in transforming the dreaded Honey Do list from a source of stress into an opportunity for growth. By mastering home improvement skills and adjusting our mindsets, we've seen how this list can strengthen relationships, enhance living spaces, build confidence, and impart valuable life lessons.

IN REVIEWING THE KEY THEMES AND TAKEAWAYS: A RECAP OF THE MAIN IDEAS

The Honey Do list is extremely common in relationships, though often unfinished and a source of frustration. Studies show that 60–75% of requested home projects on these lists go perpetually uncompleted, causing tension in many marriages and partnerships (Bob Vila, 2021). Traditionally seen as the husband's duty, these lists can provoke anxiety for men unsure of their DIY capabilities.

A lack of DIY confidence damages self-esteem but can be built up with basic skills and resources. A shocking 75% of husbands report lacking confidence in home repair skills, feeling incapable of completing their wife's requests (This Old House, 2010). But cultivating core competency around fundamental DIY techniques is within reach for any willing learner. The sense of accomplishment and self-reliance gained from successful projects is invaluable.

Investing in quality tools and learning to use them transforms project anxiety into excitement. A comprehensive toolkit allows you to take on a wide range of improvements with precision. Dedicated storage solutions like pegboards keep items organized and damage-free. With the proper equipment, even novice DIYers can build skills over time.

Prioritizing intelligently and communicating sets a collaborative tone. Openly discuss motivations, ideal timelines, and responsibilities for tasks based on abilities. Create a shared schedule for tackling items methodically as your partnership allows. Celebrate small wins to stay encouraged.

Efficiency comes from thorough planning, workspace organization, and teamwork. Declutter the work area and have materials and tools staged within reach. Work in focused batches by project type. Take breaks to recharge. Enlist an extra set of hands for complex steps. Proper preparation prevents problems down the line.

Tapping into each other's strengths and passions through cooperation lightens the workload. Teach each other new skills and split tasks based on interest, not outdated gender roles. Guidance plus patience helps generate excitement and shared pride in outcomes.

Patience and practice lead to mastery of repairs that save money over hiring contractors. Focus on easy fixes first to build fundamental proficiency. Follow online tutorials for issues like wall patching, leak fixing, sanding, and hardware repairs. Handy homeowners save an average of $330 per project (This Old House, 2023).

Curb-appeal projects build community and increase home value. A beautifully upgraded exterior boosts a home's value more than 20% (Family Handyman, 2019). It also facilitates neighborhood connections through inviting spaces to interact. Even novice DIYers can enhance curb appeal.

Teaching kids DIY skills provides bonding and valuable life lessons. Hands-on learning sticks with children, building confidence and competence. Make it fun by including them in manageable projects. Passing down these abilities creates treasured family memories and saves money later.

Reflection and celebration of wins motivates us forward. Acknowledge completed items to fuel inspiration for the next undertaking. Look back at initial hesitations overcome through guided practice. Set new goals once the current Honey Do list is under control.

This book aimed to provide men with the confidence, skills, and partnership approach to not just survive, but thrive when faced with their Honey Do list. We've covered practical strategies for completing tasks efficiently as well as cultivating the mindset to see house projects as opportunities for growth rather than burdens.

Remember, this is an ongoing journey requiring adaptation and communication. Not every skill will be mastered overnight. But by embracing DIY as a continual learning process and inviting your partner along for the ride, you can build a connection and take continual steps forward in enhancing your home and relationship.

CHAPTER TAKEAWAYS

Chapter 1

We explored the significance of the Honey Do list and its impacts on relationships. Dispelled were notions of DIY as exclusively the male's domain. Reframing projects positively and setting reasonable expectations is key.

Chapter 2

We discovered how developing fundamental DIY skills through hands-on practice boosts self-assurance and feelings of self-reliance in enhancing your home. Cultivating this DIY mindset is achievable for any willing learner.

Chapter 3

Accumulating a comprehensive toolkit allows you to take on a vast range of improvements and repairs over a lifetime. Dedicated storage solutions keep tools protected and easily accessible when needed.

Chapter 4

Open communication, pragmatic project scheduling, and celebrating small wins allows couples to methodically work through a Honey Do list together. Proper planning prevents you both from feeling overwhelmed.

Chapter 5

Thorough preparation, workspace organization, batching similar tasks, and embracing teamwork helps complete projects faster with fewer mistakes. Efficiency is achieved by working smarter, not harder.

Chapter 6

Tapping your spouse's excitement and strengths while teaching each other new skills lightens the workload. Guidance with patience builds confidence. Shared accomplishments enhance bonding.

Chapter 7

Careful practice of basic repair skills for issues like leaks, hardware, appliances, and finishes saves thousands over hiring professional contractors. Patience and online tutorials help build competence.

Chapter 8

Curb-appeal projects not only increase home value but facilitate community connections through inviting outdoor spaces. Even DIY novices can successfully enhance aesthetics.

Chapter 9

Including kids in manageable projects from a young age imparts confidence, competence, and cherished memories. Passing down DIY knowledge bonds generations.

Chapter 10

Reflecting on growth, acknowledging completed projects, and setting new goals maintains momentum. The Honey Do list is an ongoing journey requiring flexibility.

No matter your current skill level or trepidation, remember: A willingness to learn paired with a positive, communicative mindset will allow you to thrive in completing your Honey Do list. Gain courage knowing that the journey is long but achievable one step at a time. You've got this!

References

Family Handyman. (2019, April 4). Backyard ideas for creating the ultimate outdoor space. https://www.familyhandyman.com/article/backyard-ideas/

Garskof, J. (2009, January 8). 50 nifty tricks for big DIY savings. This Old House. https://www.thisoldhouse.com/21015483/50-nifty-tricks-for-big-diy-savings

Guthrie, G. (2023, September 20). Here's how to avoid a home improvement disaster. Consumer Affairs. https://www.consumeraffairs.com/news/heres-how-to-avoid-a-home-improvement-disaster-092023.html

Liu, D.K. (2023, November 12). Bonding through building: DIY projects for couples to try together. HomeTun. https://www.hometun.com/bonding-through-building-diy-projects-for-couples-to-try-together/

Lindsay. (2023, August 7). How to successfully tackle your first DIY project. My Creative Days. https://www.mycreativedays.com/how-to-successfully-tackle-your-first-diy-project/

Mosier, K. (2021, February 26). 9 Reasons why DIY is good for your well-being, according to science. Bob Vila. https://www.bobvila.com/slideshow/9-reasons-why-diy-is-good-for-your-well-being-according-to-science-579190

Nigel. (2019, February 6). Essential daddy DIY skills. DIY Daddy. https://www.diydaddyblog.com/essential-daddy-diy-skills/

Nov, D.S. (2023, November 14). 12 Home improvement ideas for beginning DIYers. Family Handyman. https://www.familyhandyman.com/list/12-home-improvement-ideas-for-beginning-diyers/

Stanley, J. (2023, August 25). 100 Home repairs you don't need to call a pro for. Family Handyman. https://www.familyhandyman.com/list/home-repairs-you-can-do-yourself/

This Old House Reviews Team. (2010, December 17). Must-have tools for every skill level. This Old House. https://www.thisoldhouse.com/tools/21018652/best-tools-for-your-home-tool-kit